You are not alone with our free Business Planning CD-ROM.

It's difficult to know where to begin when you're starting your own business. But help is at hand in the shape of our comprehensive, user-friendly CD-ROM. It takes you through your business plan preparation in a series of easy steps, giving you a focused starting point. And the price of this font of knowledge? It's free. Even if you don't bank with us. So you've got nothing to lose.

For your free copy call
0800 521 607
www.rbs.co.uk   quoting ref KO

The Royal Bank of Scotland

This book has been endorsed by the Institute of Directors.

The endorsement is given to selected Kogan Page books which the IoD recognises as being of specific interest to its members and providing them with up-to-date, informative and practical resources for creating business success. Kogan Page books endorsed by the IoD represent the most authoritative guidance available on a wide range of subjects including management, finance, marketing, training and HR.

The views expressed in this book are those of the author and are not necessarily the same as those of the Institute of Directors.

First published in 1984
Second edition published in 1988
Third edition published in 1995
Reprinted in 1997
Fourth edition published in 1998
Fifth edition published in 2001

Kogan Page Limited
120 Pentonville Road
London N1 9JN

The views expressed in this book are those of the author, and are not necessarily the same as those of Times Newspapers Ltd.

British Library Cataloguing in Publication Data

A CIP record for this book is available from the British Library.

ISBN 0 7494 3500 3

Typeset by Jean Cussons Typesetting, Diss, Norfolk
Printed and bound in Great Britain by Thanet Press Ltd, Margate

THE SUNDAY TIMES

BUSINESS ENTERPRISE GUIDE

Financial Management
for the Small Business

5TH EDITION

COLIN BARROW

RECOMMENDED BY
INSTITUTE OF DIRECTORS

KOGAN
PAGE

Contents

We don't smoke kippers

We leave that to Harry, but we were there to help him build a website when he wanted to sell his kippers online.

Whatever your business, Work24 won't tell you how to run it, but we will save you time and money, and provide you with a whole range of essential services like helping you to set up your own e-store and successfully trade online.

Work24's collective buying power also saves you money, by providing unbeatable deals on computers, stationery and business travel from the UK's leading suppliers. What's more, or rather, less, you can register now for **free!**

With the backing of two trusted companies ScottishPower and The Royal Bank of Scotland, you can be sure there's no fishy business. We leave that to Harry.

work24

Register on www.Work24.co.uk or Call 0845 2702220 today

From ScottishPower and The Royal Bank of Scotland

Preface

Since the first edition of this book, the climate for enterprise in the UK has changed profoundly. The number of self-employed individuals has risen to over 3.7 million and nearly one person in eight now works for him- or herself. This phenomenon has not been unique to the UK. The number of self-employed people in the United States had been a declining population for many years; however, in recent times, their number has risen from 7.5 million to over 11 million. Across the world the spirit of enterprise has been gaining momentum. Small businesses are being created in greater numbers everywhere, including China and former bastions of communism such as Russia and Eastern Europe. In Western Europe, 21 million people work for themselves. Every other measure of entrepreneurial activity shows a steeply rising curve: the number of venture capital organisations has risen from a few dozen boutiques to over 600 fully fledged financial institutions, some with worldwide networks. The amount they have invested in new ventures has risen correspondingly from the low hundreds of millions of pounds to over £60 billion. Europe, whilst only accounting for a third of this sum, has doubled its venture capital provision in the past two years.

Managers in larger organisations have also been swept along in the tide of entrepreneurial enthusiasm. Management buyouts, a virtually unheard of phenomenon a decade ago, now consume the lion's share of venture capital. Banks lending money to small firms and other forms of financing such as leasing, hire purchase and trade credit are at substantial and rising levels.

Alongside this sharp rise in new entrepreneurs has come an urgent need to become financially literate – an essential prerequisite for raising finance and using it wisely. Despite the recent occurrence of seemingly mindless floods of money pouring into loss-making Internet firms, it is clear that no one makes their investment with the expectation of losing their shirt. Wisely or otherwise, every Internet investment, as with every other investment or loan to a small firm, is made on the basis of a set of financial projections and a business plan that demonstrates how the venture will become profitable. Further pressure for an awareness of financial matters has been applied by the Insolvency Act and wrongful trading legislation, which make it an offence for directors to continue trading once they know – or should know – that their business is in trouble.

This book is intended to help those who find business finance confusing. A heavy fog seems to descend as soon as anyone approaches this field for the first time. Whether you are running or setting up a business, getting a first taste of responsibility for accounts or taking a business course, the first steps towards an understanding of finance are the most difficult. The consequences of failing to understand business finance are not the same for everyone. A student simply fails an exam, while a businessperson all too often loses his or her business and the executive gets fired. Competition is generally greater today and hence the margin for mistakes is smaller.

Alongside this rapid growth in entrepreneurialism has come the inevitable tide of business closures. Over 400,000 small firms close their doors each year in the UK alone. Recessions are a good test of an entrepreneur's financial skills. In the recession of the early 1990s, over 600,000 small firms a year were closing in the UK. Across Europe, over 210,000 limited companies floundered each year.

The most common cause for closure is poor financial control. Indeed, surveys of businesses routinely indicate that a third of failures are accounted for in this manner. People running small businesses frequently leave financial questions to their accountants to sort out at the end of the year. They often have the mistaken belief that keeping the books is an activity quite divorced from the 'real' task of getting customers or making the product. By the time the first set of figures is prepared by the accountant, most ailing small businesses are already too far down the road to financial failure to be saved. Even the few businesspeople who do ask for advice, perhaps from an accountant or a bank manager, often do not understand the terms being used to explain the situation. The final accounts become all too final and a good business proposition is ruined by financial illiteracy.

This book begins with an introduction to the key financial statements. All too often, these vital building blocks are missed out by those trying to get to grips with the problems of poor profits and a negative cash flow.

With this foundation, the tools of financial analysis are then explained in Part 2 – the keys to controlling a business successfully. If you can imagine trying to drive a car without any instruments at all, you will have some impression of how unsatisfactory it would be to run a business without financial controls.

Part 3 covers the field of business planning and budgeting. Most new ventures cannot get off the ground without a sound business plan and existing businesses cannot grow without one. A chapter within this section is devoted exclusively to the important task of writing up and presenting a business plan. As this is the 'ticket of entry' to capital, it is as important for the business plan to look right.

This whole book has been revised and updated to bring it right up to date – much of the material contained within this book has been used with business and academic audiences in the UK and mainland Europe over recent years. I should like to record my appreciation of those 'students' who helped me to focus on key financial issues and sharpen up my thinking generally. In particular, I am grateful to the participants of the Graduate Enterprise Programme at Stirling University, Cranfield School of Management and the Entrepreneurship Program at Suffolk University in Boston, Massachusetts, USA. Also, I would like to thank those enrolled on the small business programmes at the University of Greenwich and people attending the Royal Borough of Kensington and Chelsea's new business courses. I am also grateful to directors, executives and managers of the following companies, whose financial training programmes have included much of the material: Abbott Laboratories, Ash and Lacy, ICL, Johnson & Johnson, Leyland Paints, Seagram Distillers, Schwarzkopf, Ruberoid, the Managers Group of Companies and Wyeth Laboratories.

Success4business.com - from Lloyds TSB Business Banking

The Internet is, without doubt, the most important medium for the new decade whether for business or in our private lives. By 2003 the value of business-to-business commerce on the Internet is estimated to exceed £690 billion worldwide.

The Internet offers businesses a great opportunity to find and service customers at a much-reduced cost. What's more, it could soon be a competitive disadvantage not to have e-mail and a presence on the World Wide Web.

For many people, the prospect of using the Internet is daunting and they don't know how to use it best.

We believe it is vital for all our small and medium sized business customers (those with a turnover up to £2 million) to have the opportunity to make the most of the Internet. That's why we have developed success4business.com, our dedicated business website to help our business banking customers succeed online.

Lloyds TSB Business customers can register for success4business, but it will be of interest to anyone with a small to medium sized business. It provides access to a world of online business information, access to Internet banking and links to other useful business sites.

We are currently developing success4business.com and in time will provide its users with personalised content. Where you'll receive news, support and information that's relevant to your business, your geographical location and your interests. You'll also be able to discuss issues with other like minded businesses.

To access this dedicated business information service visit www.success4business.com.

Lloyds TSB Bank plc, 71 Lombard Street, London EC3P 3BS. Registered in England, number 2065.

Lloyds TSB Scotland plc, Henry Duncan House, 120 George Street, Edinburgh EH2 4LH. Registered in Scotland, number 95237.

Members of the Banking Ombudsman Scheme and signatories to the Banking Code.

INNOVATIVE FUNDING FOR ACQUISITIONS

The top priority for established small and medium-sized (SMEs) is that their business continues to grow. Many businesses at this stage of the business lifecycle are looking to grow organically or increasingly through acquisition. However, many find their expansion plans hampered by a lack of cashflow, and are frustrated that traditional bank funding is simply neither flexible nor imaginative enough to cope with such aspirations.

An increasing number of businesses are therefore turning to invoice discounting providers like Lloyds TSB Commercial Finance. Invoice discounting is a finance only solution that turns unpaid sales invoices into an immediate source of working capital. It is attractive in acquisition situations because instead of focusing on cashflow, credit profiles and balance sheet ratios to determine lending criteria, it considers the value of a healthy order book and sound management.

Ian Lomas, commercial director at Lloyds TSB Commercial Finance says: "There are many companies whose cashflows fluctuate. For example, a potential borrower may be in a turn-around situation or a seasonal business. In these situations, the cashflow lender might well shy away at advancing funds.

Our flexibility stems from our willingness to look at the company's track record and ahead to its future performance, understanding that although the current economic environment may not be particularly good, the business itself may well be credit-worthy."

Typically, Lloyds TSB Commercial Finance advances up to 85 per cent of book debts.

Adding the value of the debtor book as collateral allows many companies to access more capital than they could under a more traditional solution, making a real difference to the level of funds available.

Additionally, invoice discounting does not include restrictive covenants that are often imposed by more traditional financiers. Due to the high-risk nature of buy-outs, venture capitalists and business angels often issue restrictions relating to the issuing of further capital or the entering into of further transactions that will ultimately affect the future running of the business.

One of the most important considerations following an MBO is to guarantee a good source of working capital - a fact that many management teams overlook in the rush to get the deal through. This is often a problem for companies that select loan funding, as regular monthly repayments may restrict the amount of working capital available to the company during the early stages of growth.

Ian comments: "Too often deal teams overlook the importance of securing funding for a company after the deal is done. Without an ongoing supply of working capital companies will encounter difficulties financing existing orders and sales."

Again, this is where an invoice discounting facility can help. There are no monthly repayments because the service depends upon the level of the sales ledger. The service adapts to the natural growth rate of the business as the level of funding is linked to the value of the sales ledger.

Summarising the appeal of asset-based finance, Ian Lomas concludes "The uniqueness of invoice discounting is that it allows us to assess the type, quality and composition of a company's assets. It is a more dynamic route that allows the business to have more control over future financing as well as removing the need for onerous covenants."

Romford Office & Commercial Removals (ROC) is one company that has benefited from using invoice discounting. With a turnover of around £4 million, ROC operates in the area of commercial removals, storage and crate hire and has developed a national blue-chip list, which includes Marsh, Reuters and Zurich Insurance.

In August last year, the management team took the initiative to buy back the company from shareholders. The team, headed up by managing director Andy Carr turned to Roger Brown at the London office of Lloyds TSB Commercial Finance to fund the deal with an invoice discounting facility.

The decision to proceed with the MBO gave Andy and his team full control of the business and a free reign to pursue ambitious growth plans. The company has since completed a further acquisition using invoice discounting.

Andy comments: "Funding the buyout through invoice discounting discounting proved a much less restrictive form of financing. This flexibility will assist our future growth."

Number

As BK Racing discovered, if you're looking for Invoice Discounting, it's well worth taking note of our number.

An independent division of the Lloyds TSB group, we're acknowledged specialists in helping successful companies fulfil their business objectives, offering an ideal way to release the working capital that is vital for growth.

We offer a flexible range of innovative financial solutions, that can be carefully adapted to suit your individual business.

To find out how we can help you fund your ambition, call Sue Baker, on 0800 389 5084, quoting ST2.

Why let restrictive funding control your company, when, as BK Racing will confirm, we can put you back in the driving seat?

0800 389 5084

or visit our website
www.ltsbcf.co.uk

 Lloyds TSB
Commercial Finance

Smart financial solutions for growth

FACTORING FOR GROWTH

Everyone wants their business to grow, from a start-up to a company with a multimillion pound turnover, but the sad fact is that inadequate inflexible financial arrangements mean that many companies are simply not in a position to take advantage of new business opportunities that come their way.

Factoring is an ideal solution for start-ups and small to medium-sized enterprises (SMEs). A factoring company, like Alex Lawrie Factors, will free the funds locked up in a business, advancing up to 90 per cent of the value of unpaid invoices within 24-hours of raising them. The balance is available, less a small fee, when the business's customer pays.

The main benefit of factoring is the immediate cash injection to the business. Businesses can gain access to an ongoing source of funds that is linked directly to sales ensuring a smooth cashflow. It can also have a positive impact on profitability, as the business can pay suppliers earlier, buy in large quantities and also take advantage of discounts that are available.

Start-ups and SMEs also find that lack of time and dedicated in-house financial resources hold them back. As part of its factoring service, Alex Lawrie provides a credit management facility to assist in the management and collection of outstanding UK invoices. The factor will work to the client's instructions to collect their invoice payments and ensure that good customer relationships are always maintained. Businesses recognise that this relieves them from the burden of sales ledger administration, as it allows them to concentrate on other areas of their business like business development, marketing, and production.

Additionally, using a factoring facility saves costs on staff, postage, stationery and telephone calls. Essentially factoring can help client sales grow in the right way.

Alex Lawrie provides a dedicated service for companies that export their products and services. The service, which is provided either direct from its offices, or through a correspondent factoring company in the country concerned, provides all the benefits of the domestic factoring service with the option of insurance against bad debts and overseas credit checking.

Paul Saunders, commercial director at Alex Lawrie Factors, comments: "When you weigh up the cost of a business having the working capital they need at their disposal against the 'lost opportunity' cost of spending valuable time chasing unpaid bills, a factoring service makes sound financial sense. This cash injection enables an SME to fund its growth and plan its investment – a must in the early years."

One company that has benefited from using Alex Lawrie's factoring service is Reynolds Cycle. Chosen as the official supplier of the US Olympic cycle team, Midlands-based Reynolds Cycle Technology (2000), a specialist manufacturer of bicycle tubing for the top end of the racing bikes market, is a true export success story. –

Led by managing director Keith Noronha, the company has a turnover of £1.4 million and currently exports 80% of its production. In addition to developing strong ties with the North American market, its continuing success has led to strong sales in Western Europe and the Far East, dealing with leading producers, such as Trek, Schwinn/GT, Bianchi, Raleigh and Gazelle.

According to Keith Noronha, adopting an export factoring service from Alex Lawrie Factors is a key to its success. Corporate advisers, Felton & Co, recommended using factoring because of the capital intensive nature of the business. As a major exporter, they needed a simple cashflow solution that would enable it to keep its business plan on track and fund further growth.

Alex Lawrie Factors provides Reynolds with 80% of the value of unpaid invoices within 24 hours, with the remaining 20% forwarded when their customers pay. Along with a credit management facility, this allows Keith to concentrate on getting more orders and has helped in developing new products, notably a range of cutting-edge titanium and aluminium lithium alloy frames.

Keith Noronha comments: "Factoring proved the ideal solution. We can now seize greater export opportunities and diversify our product lines to ensure that we continue our substantial growth and market leadership."

not all banks are the sme

For an altogether different approach to business banking, form an alliance with us.

Now for something different. Alliance Business Banking gives you 24 hour banking by telephone, fax or the Internet. And you can bank through your local post office. Plus, if your turnover's less than £100,000 you'll pay a flat fee of only £10 per month and you will earn interest on your current account. For a bank that's on the same side as you, call Alliance Business Banking free on 0800 21 48 07 quoting reference AL0191.

Alliance Leicester

www.alliancebusinessbanking.co.uk

Part 1

Understanding key financial statements

1 *The balance sheet – where we are now*

There is a much told Irish story of the driver lost on his travels between Dublin and Cork. He stopped to ask the way of a passing farmer, who replied, 'If I were going to Cork I wouldn't start from here'.

For people in business this is an all too pertinent answer. We nearly always need a good idea of where we are now if we are to have any chance of reaching our goal. But either through pressures of more immediate tasks, or the nagging feeling that we will not like the answers, sizing up the financial situation is a job relegated to the bottom of the pile.

Even in our private lives it is helpful to 'strike a balance' when important financial issues are at stake. Questions such as should we move house, buy a boat, a new car, or take a holiday involve us in an informal sizing up of the situation before making a decision.

A personal experience

This example looks at the finances of Terry Brown. She has become a little confused by the complexity of her financial affairs and has decided to get things sorted out. In short, she wants to know where she is.

If you were to summarise your present financial position it would contain, at least, some elements of the example given in Table 1.1.

Table 1.1 Example summary of financial position

Terry Brown – Financial position today (28 March) 1

	£
Cash	50
House	50,000
Mortgage	45,000
Money owed by sister (Jackie)	135
Overdraft	100
Car (Citroën 2CV)	1,000
Credit cards	50
Jewellery and paintings	350
Hire purchase (on various goods)	500
Furniture	500

This information tells us something of Terry's circumstances, but until we organise the information we cannot really understand her true financial position.

Terry believes that in money matters things divide neatly into two: things you have and things you owe, with the latter usually exceeding the former. So, using this concept and slightly different words, we could show the same information in the following manner (Table 1.2). On the right-hand side we have made a list of Terry's *assets*: what she has done with the money she has had. On the left is listed where she got the money from to pay for these assets: the *liabilities and claims* against her.

Table 1.2 Example summary of financial position showing assets, liabilities and claims

Terry Brown – Financial position today (28 March) 2

Liabilities and claims (Where I got the money from)	£	Assets (What I have done with the money)	£
Overdraft	100	Cash	50
Mortgage	45,000	House	50,000
Hire purchase	500	Car	1,000
Credit cards	50	Jewellery and paintings	350
Total claims by other people	45,650	Money owed by sister	135
My capital	6,385	Furniture	500
Total of my and other people's money	52,035	My assets	52,035

You may have got a little lost towards the bottom of the left-hand column. This is simply because we have to try and show the complete picture of Terry's financial affairs. She has acquired £52,035 worth of assets and must have provided an identical sum from one source or another. We can find only £45,650 owed to other people. The only reasonable assumption is that Terry herself must have put in the balance over the past years. In other words, she has put her past salary or wages towards buying the assets.

Now while Terry might be happy with the help we have given her so far, it is unlikely she will be completely satisfied. Like the rest of us, she probably considers events as long- or short-term in nature. Even though we have shown a fairly dazzling picture of £50,000+ of assets, she knows she is short of cash for day-to-day living. So once again we could restructure the information on her financial position to give a clearer picture (Table 1.3).

For example, we can now see that her short-term financial position is dominated by the money her sister owes her. If that is safe, then all

Table 1.3 Example summary of financial position showing long- and short-term assets, liabilities and claims

Terry Brown – Financial position today (28 March) 3

Liabilities (long term)		Fixed assets (long term)	
(Where I got the money from)		(What have I done with the money)	
	£		£
Mortgage	45,000	House	50,000
Hire purchase	500	Car	1,000
		Furniture	500
My capital	6,385	Jewellery and paintings	350
	51,885		51,850
Current liabilities (short term)		Current assets (short term)	
Overdraft	100	Money owed by sister	135
Credit cards	50	Cash	50
	150		185
Total liabilities	52,035	Total assets	52,035

current liabilities can be met. If it is not safe, and that money is unlikely to be repaid quickly, the position is not to good. There is an accounting convention according to which 'current' liabilities are those that we will have to pay within a year. Similarly, 'current' assets will turn into cash within a year.

We are getting very close to having a *balance sheet* of Terry's financial position. One further adjustment will reveal all. It is vital that both the long- and short-term financial positions are readily visible to the examiner. Terry's day-to-day assets and liabilities need to be clearly highlighted. What we are looking for is the net position: how much she currently owes, subtracted from how much she has.

By redrafting the financial position, we shall see the whole picture more clearly (Table 1.4). £51,850 is tied up in *fixed assets* and £35 is tied up in *net current assets*. All these have been *financed by* £6,385 of Terry's capital and £45,500 which has been provided by a mortgage and a hire purchase company.

IT ALL ADDS UP

HIGH INTEREST – GUARANTEED

Our Fixed Rate Bonds offer a safe and worry-free home for your savings.

At the same time they pay amongst the highest interest rates in the country. And we guarantee you the same rate for the term of your deposit – from six months to five years.

So call the freephone number below now for a complete list of interest rates and deposit periods.

0800 279 9880

Please quote: STFM

PROVIDIAN
National Bank

Table 1.4   Example balance sheet

Terry Brown – Balance sheet 28 March

Fixed assets		£
House		50,000
Car		1,000
Furniture		500
Jewellery and paintings		350
		51,850
Current assets		
Money owed by sister		135
Cash		50
		185
Less Current liabilities		
Overdraft		100
Credit cards		50
		150
So, Net current assets		35
Total assets, *less* Current liabilities		51,885
Financed by		
My capital		6,385
Mortgage	45,000	
Hire purchase	500	45,500
Total		51,885

The public picture

Terry Brown found it useful to have a clear picture of her current financial position. A business will find such a picture essential. While most people are responsible only to themselves and their families, businesses have a wider audience. Partners, bankers, shareholders, financial institutions, Customs and Excise and the Inland Revenue are only a few of the possible interested parties, apart from the owners' and managers' interest in the financial situation which is taken for granted.

All these interested parties keep track of a business's financial performance by having a series of reports, or statements, prepared. In effect a business acts as a steward of other people's money and it is to give account of this stewardship that these financial records are prepared. While these 'figure' statements provide usual evidence, it is as well to remember that the evidence is only partial: nothing in Terry's balance sheet has told us that she is shapely, 27 years old and currently sporting a carrot-red head of hair.

Another important limitation on these financial statements is the reliability of the figures themselves. The cash-in-hand figure is probably dead right, but can the same be said of the furniture values? Accountants have their own rules on how these figures are to be arrived at, but they do not pretend to anything better than an approximation. Every measuring device has inherent inaccuracies, and financial controls are no exception.

Not all the information that we need to prepare a financial statement is always readily on hand. For example, Terry has not had a statement on her credit card account since February (the preceding month), so despite the incomplete data, she has made an educated guess at the current position.

With these questions of reliability in mind, let us now look at how a business monitors and controls its financial position.

The structure of the business balance sheet

You might have noticed that we stopped calling Terry's statement a financial position, and called it a balance sheet in the last example. This is one of the principal business control reports. It is designed to show what assets the business is using at a particular time, and where it got the money to finance those assets. The balance sheet is usually a statement of the present position, but, of course, once a business has been in existence for some time there will be historical balance sheets. These can be used to compare performance in one year (period) with another. This use of the balance sheet will be examined in the chapters on financial control.

It is also possible to prepare a projected balance sheet to show what the future financial picture might look like, given certain assumptions. We shall look at this aspect in more detail in the chapters on planning and budgeting.

You will notice a number of differences between the business balance sheet in Table 1.5 and the personal one we looked at before. But there are also many basic similarities.

First, you will notice the date at the top. This is essential, as the balance sheet is a picture of the business at a particular moment in time. The picture could look quite different tomorrow if, for example, some of the £400 cash was spent on further fixtures and fittings. There are three columns of £s simply to make the arithmetic of the subtotals easier to calculate and understand.

You can also see that some different terms are used for the account categories. Before looking at the main elements of this balance sheet it will be useful to describe the key terms, assets and liabilities.

A balance sheet for a small business might look something like Table 1.5.

Table 1.5   Example balance sheet for a small business

Balance sheet at 31 December, year _____

Net assets employed	£	£	£
Fixed assets			
Equipment/machinery		9,000	
Fixtures and fittings		3,800	12,800
Current assets			
Stock	700		
Debtors	700		
Cash	400	1,800	
Less Current liabilities			
Creditors		900	
Net current assets			
(Working capital)			900
			13,700
Financed by			
Owner's capital introduced	6,500		
Add Net profit for year	5,000		
	11,500		
Less Drawings	4,500		7,000
10-year loan from bank			6,700
			13,700

Assets

Accountants describe assets as 'valuable resources, owned by a business, which were accrued at a measurable money cost'. You can see that there are three key points in the definition:

1. To be valuable the resource must be cash, or of some use in generating current or future profits. For example, a debtor (someone who owes a business money for goods or services provided) usually pays up. When he or she does, the debtor becomes cash and so meets this test. If there is no hope of getting payment then you can hardly view the sum as an asset.
2. Ownership, in its legal sense, can be seen as different from possession or control. The accounting use of the word is similar but not identical. In a business, possession and control are not enough to make a resource an asset. For example, a leased machine may be possessed and controlled by a business but be owned by the leasing company. So not only is it not an asset, it is a regular expense. (More about expenses in the next chapter.)
3. Most business resources are bought for a 'measurable money cost'. Often this test is all too painfully obvious. If you pay cash for something, or promise to pay at a later date, it is clearly an asset. If the resource was manufactured by the business, then money was paid in wages, materials, etc during that process. There may be problems in deciding exactly what money figure to put down, but there is no problem in seeing that money has been spent.

The asset 'goodwill' is one important grey area of particular interest to those buying or selling a small business.

Ranking of assets

There is a useful convention that recommends listing assets in the balance sheet in their order of permanence, that is, starting out with the most difficult to turn into cash and working down to cash itself. This structure is very practical when you are looking at someone else's balance sheet, or comparing balance sheets. It can also help you to recognise obvious information gaps quickly.

Liabilities

These are the claims by people outside the business. In our examples only creditors are shown, but they could include such items as: tax; accruals; deferred income; overdrafts, etc. The 'financed by' section of our example balance sheet is considered in part as liabilities.

Current

This is the term used with both assets and liabilities to show that they will be converted into cash, or have a short life (under one year).

Now let's go through the main elements of the balance sheet.

Net assets employed

This is the 'What have we done with the money?' section. A business can only do three things with funds:

1. It can buy *fixed assets*, such as premises, machinery and motor cars. These are assets that the business intends to keep over the longer term. They will be used to help make profits, but will not physically vanish in the short term (unless sold and replaced, like motor cars, for example).
2. Money can be tied up in *working capital*, that is, 'things' immediately involved in the business's products (or services) that will vanish in the short term. Stocks get sold and are replaced; debtors pay up, and creditors are paid; and cash circulates. Working capital is calculated by subtracting the current liabilities from the current assets. This is the net sum of money that a business has to find to finance the working capital. In the balance sheet this is called the *net current assets*, but on most other occasions the term working capital is used.
3. Finally, a business can put money aside over the longer term, perhaps in local government bonds or as an investment in someone else's business venture. In the latter case this could be a prelude to takeover. In the former it could be a cash reserve for future capital investment. The account category is called *investments*. It is not shown in this example as it is a fairly rare phenomenon in new or small businesses, which are usually cash hungry rather than rich.

SELF-EMPLOYED MORTGAGES MADE SIMPLE

Charles Reed, MD of UCB Home Loans, the specialist lender of Nationwide Building Society, looks at mortgages for the self-employed.

So you're self-employed and are looking for a mortgage? What can you expect from lenders when it comes to accepting you for a mortgage and the amount that they are prepared to lend?

Assessing your income

Lenders have many different ways of assessing your income when you're self-employed, most of which are centred around a review of your accounts. This may be fine if you have a successful company with an endless list of repeat orders or you have been in business for years, but what if you haven't?

Sole traders, partnerships and small limited companies may not always have a steady flow of business - everybody has experienced good and bad years of trading. Traditional lenders will naturally take this into account when assessing your accounts, but it may affect the level of borrowing available. Lenders may want to review up to 3 years of your business accounts, compiled by a Chartered or Certified Accountant. They will look at your turnover, costs and net profit to establish whether, in their view, your business is growing and able to cover the mortgage you have applied for. However, traditional lenders are not your only option, there are specialist lenders that cater specifically for your needs.

Self-certification

If you're looking for a forward thinking attitude towards mortgage lending then UCB Home Loans can help. Instead of dissecting your accounts to establish how much you can borrow, we simply ask you to tell us how much you earn and we base the mortgage on that figure. We call our approach 'self-certification lending', as you are certifying your own income. As long as you have been trading for one year or more and have a good credit history, you can typically borrow up to 3.25 times your income plus a partner's income, or 2.75 times your combined joint incomes, to purchase or remortgage your home.

Getting the best deal

Whether you are looking to buy a home, or remortgage for home improvements, a major purchase or to raise capital for your business, you will need to ensure that you get a good deal that suits you and your future plans.

You can expect a wide range of competitive products including fixed, variable, discounted or flexible mortgages and will be offered advice by specially trained consultants who understand your needs and will help you decide on the mortgage that best suits your circumstances.

Perfect products

According to research by the Council of Mortgage Lenders (CML), a quarter of self-employed borrowers opt for a flexible mortgage, around ten per cent higher than the national average. UCB Home Loans' FlexiPlus mortgage appeals to the self-employed because the features allow you to take control of your finances and make your money work harder for you. This is achieved through features such as overpayments, to help you repay your mortgage faster and potentially save thousands of pounds - and, of course, interest is calculated daily to ensure that you get the maximum benefit from any overpayments made. If you have Internet access you can log on at www.ucbhomeloans.co.uk and use our FlexiPlus calculator to see for yourself how much you could save. Other features include payment holidays to help you cope with times of high expenditure or lower income. Our credit reserve facility is also useful as it provides quick and easy access to guaranteed additional funds. This means that you could raise business capital on your home instead of borrowing at business rates and repay it, without charge, when you no longer need it.

UCB Home Loans also offers a Buy2Let mortgage for private investors who want to become landlords. Buying a property to let should be considered as a long-term investment proposition, but there is still plenty of scope for a good return on the capital invested. The mortgage is calculated on both personal earnings and projected rental income, allowing more flexibility when calculating the amount of mortgage available, and with a three year discounted rate on offer there is even more reason to think seriously about buying a property to let.

Make contact

If UCB Home Loans sounds like the type of lender you should be talking to, make contact today by calling one of our personal mortgage consultants on 0845 950 1500 or logging onto www.ucbhomeloans.co.uk to make your next mortgage move a simple one.

Financed by

This section of the balance sheet shows where the money came from. It usually has at least three subheadings, although larger companies can have many more.

1. The *owner's capital introduced* shows the money put into the business by the proprietor. If this was the balance sheet of a limited company it would be called *share capital*. There could then follow a list of different types of share, for example, preference and ordinary shares.

2. The second source of funds is the *profits* ploughed back into the business to help it grow. In this example the £5,000 profit was reduced to £500 after the owner had taken his drawings – or wages – out. So £500 was *retained* and this is the term often used to describe this ploughed-back profit. Another term in common use is *reserves*, which conjures up pictures of sums of cash stored away for a rainy day. It is important to remember that this is not necessarily so. The only cash in a business is that shown under that heading in the current assets. The reserves, like all the other funds, are used to finance a business and are tied up in fixed assets and working capital.

3. The final source of money to finance a business is long-term *loans* from outside parties. These loans could be in the form of debentures, a mortgage, hire purchase agreements or long-term loans from a bank. The common features of all such loans are that businesses have to pay interest on the money, and eventually repay the capital whether or not the business is successful. Conversely, if the business is a spectacular success the lenders, unlike the shareholders, will not share in the extra profits.

The ground rules, concepts and conventions

Accounting is certainly not an exact science. Even the most enthusiastic member of the profession would not make that claim. As we have already seen, there is considerable scope for interpretation and educated guesswork. Obviously, if this were to go on unbridled no one inside or outside the business would place any reliance on the figures, so certain ground rules have been laid down by the profession to help get a level of consistency into accounting information.

1. *Money measurement.* In accounting, a record is kept only of the facts that can be expressed in money terms. For example, the state of the managing director's health and the news that your main competitor is opening up right opposite in a more attractive outlet are important business facts. No accounting record of them is made, however, and they do not show up on the balance sheet, simply because no objective monetary value can be assigned to these facts.

   Expressing business facts in money terms has the great advantage of providing a common denominator. Just imagine trying to add typewriters and motor cars, together with a 4,000 square foot workshop, and then arriving at a total. You need a common term to be able to carry out the basic arithmetical functions, and to compare one set of accounts with another.

   There is one great danger with expressing things in money terms. It suggests that all the pounds are identical. This is not always so. Pounds currently shown as cash in a balance sheet are not exactly the same, for example, as debtors' pounds that may not be turned into cash for many months. The ways of examining this changing value of money over time are looked at in Chapter 7.

2. *Business entity.* The accounts are kept for the business itself, rather than for the owner(s), workers, or anyone else associated with the firm. If an owner puts a short-term cash injection into his business, it will appear as a loan under current liabilities in the business account. In his personal account it will appear as an asset – money someone else owes him. So depending on which point of view you take, the same sum of money can be an asset or a liability. And as in this example the owner and the business are substantially the same person, the possibilities of confusion are considerable. This source of possible confusion must be cleared up and the business entity concept does just that.

   The concept states that assets and liabilities are always defined from the business's viewpoint. Once again it is this idea of stewardship that forces us to see the business as an entity separate from *all* outside parties.

3. *Cost concept*. Assets are usually entered into the accounts at cost. For a variety of reasons, the real 'worth' of an asset will probably change over time.

   The worth, or value, of an asset is a subjective estimate which no two people are likely to agree on. This is made even more complex, and artificial, because the assets themselves are usually not for sale. So in the search for objectivity, the accountants have settled for cost as the figure to record. It does mean that a balance sheet does not show the current worth or value of a business. That is not its intention. Nor does it mean that the 'cost' figure remains unchanged forever. For example, a motor car costing £6,000 may end up looking like this (Table 1.6) after two years:

Table 1.6   Example of the changing worth of an asset

Year 1		*Year 2*	
Fixed assets	£	Fixed assets	£
Motor car	6,000	Motor car	6,000
Less cumulative depreciation	1,500	*Less* cumulative depreciation	3,000
Net asset	4,500	Net asset	3,000

The depreciation is how we show the asset being 'consumed' over its working life. It is simply a bookkeeping record to allow us to allocate some of the cost of an asset to the appropriate time period. The time period will be determined by factors such as the working life of the asset. The Inland Revenue does not allow depreciation as a business expense – but it does allow tax relief on the capital expenditure. The proportion of capital purchase allowed by the Inland Revenue to be offset against tax is called the 'writing down' or 'capital allowance'. It is generally 25 per cent of the declining balance; in other words, in year one you can write down £250 on a capital purchase of £1,000, in year two £188 (25 per cent of £750) and so on. However, currently small and medium-sized firms are allowed to write down 40 per cent (but not on cars or assets for leasing). This measure was intended to stimulate capital expenditure.

Other assets, such as freehold land and buildings, will be revalued from time to time, and stock will be entered at cost, or market value, whichever is the lower, in line with the principle of conservatism (explained on page 20).

4. *Going concern.* Accounting reports always assume that a business will continue trading indefinitely into the future – unless there is good evidence to the contrary. This means that the assets of the business are looked at simply as profit generators and not as being available for sale.

Look again at the motor car example above. In year 2, the net asset figures in the accounts, prepared on a 'going concern' basis, is £3,000. If we knew that the business was to close down in a few weeks, then we would be more interested in the car's resale value than its 'book' value: the car might fetch only £2,000, which is quite a different figure.

Once a business stops trading, we cannot realistically look at the assets in the same way. They are no longer being used in the business to help generate sales and profits. The most objective figure is what they might realise in the marketplace. Anyone who has been to a sale of machinery will know the difference between book and market value!

5. *Dual aspect.* To keep a complete record of any business transaction we need to know both where money came from and what has been done with it. It is not enough simply to say, for example, that someone has put £1,000 into their business. We have to see how that money has been used.

Take a look at the example in Table 1.7. Column 1 contains the figures we inherited before the owner put an extra £1,000 into the business. Column 2 shows what happened to the 'financed by' section of the balance sheet at the moment more money was put in. But as you can see, the balance sheet does not balance. It is also logically clear that we must have done something with that £1,000 the moment we received it. Column 3 shows exactly how we have used the money. It is tied up in cash. It could just as easily have been used to finance more customers (debtors) or to buy more stock, or even to pay off a bill, ie reduce creditors.

Table 1.7   An example of balance sheet changes

Net assets employed	1		2		3	
	£	£	£	£	£	£
Fixed assets		12,800		12,800		12,800
Current assets						
Stock	700		700		700	
Debtors	700		700		700	
Cash	400		400		1,400	
	1,800		1,800		2,800	
Less current liabilities						
Creditors	(900)		(900)		(900)	
Net current assets		900		900		1,900
		13,700		13,700		14,700
Financed by						
Owner's capital (less drawings)		7,000		8,000		8,000
10-year loan from bank		6,700		6,700		6,700
		13,700		14,700		14,700

However, the essential relationship of 'Assets = Capital + Liabilities' has to be maintained. That is the basis of double-entry bookkeeping. You can think of it as the accounting equivalent of Newton's third law: 'For every force there is an equal and opposite reaction'.

There are two other important accounting concepts, realisation and accrual, but they can be better dealt with when the next accounting report is looked at.

Accounting conventions

These concepts provide a useful set of ground rules, but they are open to a range of possible interpretations. Over time, a generally accepted approach to how the concepts are applied has been arrived at. This approach hinges on the use of three conventions: conservatism, materiality and consistency.

Conservatism

Accountants are often viewed as merchants of gloom, always prone to take a pessimistic point of view. The fact that a point of view has to be taken at all is the root of the problem. The convention of conservatism means that, given a choice, the accountant takes the figure that will result in a lower end profit. This might mean, for example, taking the higher of two possible expense figures. Few people are upset if the profit figure at the end of the day is higher than earlier estimates. The converse is never true.

Materiality

A strict interpretation of depreciation (see *cost concept*, item 3, on page 17) would lead to all sorts of trivial paperwork. For example, pencil sharpeners, staplers and paperclips, all theoretically items of fixed assets, should be depreciated over their working lives. This is obviously a useless exercise and in practice these items are written off when they are bought.

Clearly, the level of 'materiality' is not the same for all businesses. A multinational may not keep meticulous records of every item of machinery under £1,000. For a small business this may represent all the machinery it has.

Consistency

Even with the help of those concepts and conventions, there is a fair degree of latitude in how you can record and interpret financial information. You should choose the methods that give the fairest picture of how the firm is performing and stick with them. It is very difficult to keep track of events in a business that is always changing its accounting methods. This does not mean that you are stuck with one method for ever. Any change, however, is an important step.

The balance sheet shown earlier, though very simple, is complete enough to demonstrate the key principles involved. A much larger or more complex business may have more account categories, but the main sections of its balance sheet will be much the same, and you will now be able to recognise them.

Questions

These questions may help you to make sure of your understanding of the balance sheet.

1. Draw up your own personal balance sheet, using the four stages of the Terry Brown example as your guide.
2. A friend has brought round the following information about his business and asked for your help. Put together a balance sheet for him.

The situation today (Sunday 24 April)

	£
Debtors	1,400
Creditors	1,800
Factory premises	18,000
Cash in hand	800
Tax due to be paid	700
(should have gone out last week)	
Equipment and machinery	7,600
Money I put in at start	18,700
Long-term loan	12,000
Money I have drawn out so far	4,000
Stock	1,400

It's time to look after No.1 for a change

In the past four years we've saved investors over £14 million in returned commissions and discounted charges on ISAs, pensions and other investments.

If you invest £7000 in a big name ISA, you could receive a rebate of up to £350* if you send your application via Torquil Clark. We charge just one flat fee of £25. Similarly, if you know the pension you're looking for, you can pay one straight fee of only £50 (plus VAT) and be secure in the knowledge that you will avoid paying unnecessary commission as well as benefiting from huge reductions in charges.

You'll find that with Torquil Clark you can get much better value than if you go direct. For a free brochure and guide call our Freephone number or visit our website.

Torquil Clark. Your first choice for better value investments.

0800 413186

www.tqonline.co.uk

TORQUIL CLARK plc
The value brokers

Torquil Clark plc, St Mark's, Chapel Ash, Wolverhampton, WV3 OTZ

A NEW ERA

The way we all buy financial products is changing. Taking five minutes to read and understand this short piece, on something I like to call 'value broking', could be invaluable to you over the years. It's a straightforward concept, which is taking off in the UK. It's been pioneered by my own company, Torquil Clark plc.

Back in the olden days, insurance companies hit upon the idea of taking on sales agents to push their policies onto an unsuspecting public. They (the insurance companies) soon worked out that if they paid commission to these agents, then they would sell more policies, and eventually commission rates rose so much that the amounts became almost ludicrous. Nowadays, financial advisers and insurance company salesmen can earn thousands of pounds at a time when they sell you their pensions, investments and life policies.

Now we all like the idea of our money not going to waste, and this is particularly true of the 'smaller' business person, for whom the constant pressure to earn more than his/her business spends is unrelenting, and ever more acute in this increasingly competitive world.

The fact is that financial products, those pensions, investments and life policies which are taken out by thousands of people across the UK each day, cost you and I much more than they need to. The household name companies who sell you their financial wares are far from keen to let you have the full story, and are expert in disguising the way they take their charges and commissions from, say, your pension plan, whose explanatory leaflet could perhaps be deciphered by the odd specialist actuary, but not by the person who will actually be paying the money in; you!

So the ISA you invest in to save for the future, the pension you start to ensure a decent retirement, or the life policy you take out to protect your family and liabilities, all end up being quite expensive, largely due to commission.

In 1994 Torquil Clark launched a ground-breaking dealing service. We decided that,

if you have a good idea which investment you wish to buy, we could afford to set it up without taking the initial commission which is built into the initial charge which you usually pay. We could afford to do this because we weren't spending time advising you on the best course of action; we were simply offering you a processing service. We would usually charge you a small processing fee, typically £25, but the savings you could make would often be hundreds of pounds.

This concept of 'value broking', as I like to call it, is therefore simply a low-cost dealing service for ordinary investors. It enables you to buy the very same products that you see advertised in the press, or on TV or radio, but at a much lower cost. Sometimes we will pay you a cashback payment after you have invested, or sometimes we will just reduce the initial charges which the product provider would normally levy. We can deal in most of the mainstream financial products that people buy every day of the week.

So, as you are in business, you will need to set up pension arrangements. You are, of course, free to go directly to a pension company or financial adviser and pay their going rates of charges, probably unaware of their full effect. Doing it through Torquil Clark's value broking team will, almost certainly, ensure that the charges and commissions taken out of your pension funds will be considerably lower, with the direct consequence being a much bigger pension fund when you retire. If you need to buy any life assurance, Torquil Clark can give you an extremely competitively priced product, and then, incredibly, a cashback equivalent to up to a year's premiums. And investments like ISAs, unit trusts and investment bonds are also much cheaper through Torquil Clark.

Torquil Clark is at the forefront of value broking. We can send you an information pack if you give them a call on 0800 413186, or visit our website at
www.tqonline.co.uk
<http://www.tqonline.co.uk>.

Torquil Clark is regulated by the Personal Investment Authority.

2

The profit-and-loss account – where we have been

The balance sheet shows the financial position of a business at a particular moment in time. Over time that picture will change, just as pictures of you, first as a baby, then as a teenager and lastly as an adult, will all be different – but nevertheless true likenesses of you. The 'ageing' process that changes a business's appearance is an event called a 'transaction'. This takes place when anything is done that can be represented in money terms. For example, if you buy in stock, sell out to a customer or take credit, these are all events that can be expressed in money.

Dealing with transactions

Let us take a very simple example. On 6 April a new business called High Finance Limited is started. The initial share capital is £10,000 and on day 1 this money is held in the company's bank. The balance sheet would look something like Table 2.1.

Table 2.1 Example balance sheet for High Finance 1

Balance sheet for High Finance Ltd at 6 April, year _____

Assets employed	£
Cash at bank	10,000
Financed by	
Share capital	10,000

Not very profound, but it does show the true picture at that date. On 7 April things begin to happen (see Table 2.2).

Table 2.2 Example balance sheet for High Finance 2

Balance sheet for High Finance Ltd at 7 April, year _____

Assets employed	£	£
Current assets		
Cash at Bank A and in hand	15,000	
Less Current liabilities		
Overdraft (Bank B)	5,000	
Net current assets		10,000
Financed by		
Share capital		10,000

High Finance borrows £5,000 on an overdraft from another bank, taking the money out immediately in cash. This event is an accounting transaction and the new balance sheet is shown above.

You can see that the asset, 'cash', has gone up, and the liability, 'overdraft', has also risen. Any financial event must have at least two effects on the balance sheet.

On 8 April, High Finance buys in stock for resale at a cost of £2,000, paying cash (Table 2.3).

Table 2.3 Example balance sheet for High Finance 3

Balance sheet for High Finance Ltd at 8 April, year _____

Assets employed	£	£
Current assets		
Cash at bank and in hand	13,000	
Stock	2,000	
	15,000	
Less Current liabilities		
Overdraft	5,000	
Net current assets		10,000
Financed by		
Share capital		10,000

The working capital has been changed, not in total, but in content. Cash has been reduced to pay for stock. However, a new asset, stock, has been acquired.

On 9 April, High Finance sells for £300 cash, stock that cost it £200.

Table 2.4 Example balance sheet for High Finance 4

Balance sheet for High Finance Ltd at 9 April, year _____

Assets employed	£	£
Currents assets		
Cash at bank and in hand	13,300	
Stock	1,800	
	15,100	
Less Current liabilities		
Overdraft	5,000	
Net current assets		10,100
Financed by		
Share capital	10,000	
Retained earnings (reserves)	100	
		10,100

In this case cash has been increased by £300, the money received from a customer. Stocks have been reduced by £200, the amount sold. Finally, a 'profit' has been made and this can be shown, at least in this example, as *retained earnings* (or reserves).

The residential effect of *all* trading transactions is an increase or decrease in the worth of the business to the owners (shareholders in this case). Income from sales tends to increase the worth of a business. Expenses incurred in generating sales tend to decrease the worth. These events are so vital to the business that they are all monitored in a separate accounting report – the *profit-and-loss account*.

So to summarise: the balance sheet shows the financial picture of a business at a particular moment in time. The profit-and-loss account monitors income and expenditure over a particular period of time. The time intervals can be a week, a month, an accounting period, or a year. While we are very interested in all the components of income and expenditure, it is the result, the net profit (or loss), that we are most interested in. This shows the increase (or decrease) in the business's worth, over the time in question.

Some more ground rules

Before looking at the structure of the profit-and-loss account it would be helpful to look at the accounting concepts that apply to it. These are numbered 6 and 7 to follow on from the five concepts given on pages 16–19 in Chapter 1.

6. *The realisation concept.* A particularly prudent sales manager once said that an order was not an order until the customer's cheque had cleared, he or she had consumed the product, had not died as a result, and, finally, had shown every indication of wanting to buy again.

Most of us know quite different salespeople who can 'anticipate' the most unlikely volume of sales. In accounting, income is usually recognised as having been earned when the goods (or services) are dispatched and the invoice sent out. This has nothing to do with when an order is received, how firm an order is or how likely a customer is to pay up promptly.

It is also possible that some of the products dispatched may be returned at some later date – perhaps for quality reasons. This means that income, and consequently profit, can be brought into the business in one period, and have to be removed later on. Obviously, if these returns can be estimated accurately, then an adjustment can be made to income at the time.

So the 'sales income' figure that is seen at the top of a profit-and-loss account is the value of the goods dispatched and invoiced to customers in the period in question.

7. *The accrual concept.* The profit-and-loss account sets out to 'match' income and expenditure to the appropriate time period. It is only in this way that the profit for the period can be realistically calculated. Suppose, for example, that you are calculating one month's profits when the quarterly telephone bill comes in. The picture might look like Table 2.5.

Table 2.5 Example of a badly matched profit-and-loss account

Profit-and-loss account for January, year _____

	£
Sales income for January	4,000
Less telephone bill (last quarter)	800
Profit	3,200

This is clearly wrong. In the first place, three months' telephone charges have been 'matched' against one month's sales. Equally wrong is charging anything other than January's telephone bill against January's income. Unfortunately, bills such as this are rarely to hand when you want the accounts, so in practice the telephone bill is 'accrued' for. The figure (which may even be absolutely correct if you have a meter) is put in as a provision to meet this liability when it becomes due.

With these two additional concepts we can now look at a business profit-and-loss account (Table 2.6).

Profit-and-loss account for a manufacturing business

Table 2.6 Example of a profit-and-loss account for a small manufacturing company

Hardcourt Ltd
Profit-and-loss account for the year ended 31 December

	£
Sales	100,000
Cost of goods sold	65,000
Gross profit	35,000
Selling expenses	5,000
Administrative expenses	14,000
Total expenses	19,000
Net profit before tax	16,000
Tax at 25%	4,000
Net profit after tax	12,000

This is a simplified profit-and-loss account for a small manufacturing company. A glance at it will show that we have at least three sorts of profit to measure in it. The first, *gross profit*, is the difference between the sales income that we have generated and all the costs that have gone into making the goods (see Table 2.7).

Table 2.7   Example of a profit-and-loss account for a small manufacturing company including cost of goods sold

Hardcourt Ltd
Profit-and-loss account for the year ended 31 December

	£	£	£
Sales			100,000
Manufacturing costs			
Raw materials opening stock	30,000		
Purchases in period	25,000		
	55,000		
Less Raw materials closing stock	15,500		
Cost of materials used		39,500	
Direct labour cost		18,000	
Manufacturing overhead cost			
Indirect labour	4,000		
Workshop heat, light and power	3,500		
Total manufacturing costs		7,500	
Cost of goods sold			65,000
Gross profit			35,000

Cost of goods sold

Now you may consider that everything you have spent in the business has gone into 'making' the product, but to calculate the cost of goods sold, only costs strictly concerned with making are considered. These will include the cost of all materials and the cost of manufacturing labour.

After blowing up the cost of goods sold section, Hardcourt's profit-and-loss account could look like Table 2.7.

This is not a complete list of items we would find in the cost of goods sold section of a manufacturer's profit-and-loss account. For example, work in progress, plant depreciation, etc have been ignored to keep the example clear enough for the principle to be established.

Net profit before and after tax

The second type of profit we have to measure is net profit before tax (NPBT). This is arrived at by deducting all the other expenses from the gross profit. The final item to be deducted is tax, which leaves the last profit to be measured, net profit after tax (NPAT), or the much-referred-to 'bottom line'.

Clearly, we could arrive at net profit after tax by simply deducting all the expenses for the period from all the income. The reason for 'organising' the information is to help us analyse and interpret that information: in other words, to see how we made a certain profit or loss in a particular trading period.

Profit-and-loss account for a service business

All the basic principles and practices of the manufacturing business apply to a service or professional business. The main area of difference will be in the calculation of gross profit. For example, a consultancy organisation's profit-and-loss account could look like Table 2.8.

Table 2.8   Example of a consultancy organisation's profit-and-loss account

Thames Consultants

	£	£
Sales	65,000	
Fees paid to consultants	30,000	
Profit before expenses (gross profit)		35,000
Expenses, etc (as for any other business)	...	

Or a travel agency's account might like like Table 2.9.

Table 2.9   Example of a travel agency's profit-and-loss account

Sunburn Travel

	£
Sales	200,000
Payments to carriers	130,000
Net commission income (gross profit)	70,000
Expenses, etc (as for any other business)	...

You can see that the basic principle of calculating the gross profit, or the margin that is left after the cost of 'producing' the service has been met, is being maintained.

Sales analysis

It may be useful to show the sales revenue by each major product group (Table 2.10), and by home and export sales, if appropriate. It would be even more useful to show the gross margin by major product.

Table 2.10   Example of a profit-and-loss account showing sales revenue of different products

Domestic Furniture Ltd

Sales:	£	£
Tables	50,000	
Chairs	20,000	
Repairs, etc	10,000	
		80,000
Cost of goods sold		50,000
Gross profit		30,000
Less expenses (as for any other business)		...

The structure of a profit-and-loss account

Once a business has been trading for a few years it will have taken on a wide range of new commitments. For example, as well as the owner's money, there may be a long-term loan to be serviced (interest and capital repayments), or parts of the workshop or offices may be sublet. Now the business profit-and-loss account will include most of the elements in the example in Table 2.11.

Like any accounting report it should be prepared in the best form for the user. The elements of this example are explained below.

1. Sales (and any other revenues from operations).
2. Cost of sales (or cost of goods sold). (At the moment a product is sold and its income is 'realised', so too are its costs.) See fuller explanation of cost of goods sold on page 31.
3. Gross profit – the difference between sales and cost of sales.
4. Operating expenses – selling, administration and general.
5. Operating profit – the difference between gross profit and operating expenses.
6. Non-operating revenues – other revenues, including interest, rent, etc.
7. Non-operating expenses – financial costs and other expenses not directly related to the running of the business.
8. Profit before income tax.
9. Provision for income tax.
10. Net income (or profit or loss).

Just to make sure you understand the process and structure of the profit-and-loss account, work through the examples at the end of the chapter.

Table 2.11 Example showing the structure of a profit-and-loss account

Profit-and-loss account

		£	£
1.	Sales		140,000
2.	Cost of sales		
	Opening stock	18,000	
	Purchases	74,000	
		92,000	
	Less Closing stock	22,000	
	Cost of goods sold		70,000
3.	Gross profit		70,000
4.	Operating expenses		
	Selling	12,500	
	Administration	12,500	
	General	30,000	
	Total expenses		55,000
5.	Operating (or trading) profit		15,000
6.	Non-operating revenue		
	Investment interest	1,000	
	Rents	500	
	Total		1,500
			16,500
7.	Non-operating expenses		
	Loan interest paid		3,000
8.	Profit before income tax		13,500
9.	Tax at 25%		3,375
10.	Profit after tax		10,125
	Opening stock	18,000	
	Plus Purchases	74,000	
	Equals Goods available for sale	92,000	
	Less Closing stock	22,000	
	Cost of goods sold	70,000	

Accounting requirements of the Companies Acts

A very sizeable majority of small businesses are either sole traders or partnerships. Such businesses have some latitude as to how they show their accounts, but obviously they would be prudent to follow guidelines such as those in these first two chapters.

Limited companies do have to prepare accounts and file them with the Registrar of Companies. The Companies Act 1985 laid down standard balance sheet and profit-and-loss account formats, and various later Companies Acts have modified these. The formats are similar to those we have been looking at, but by no means as clear and understandable to the layman, as they are really designed for company auditors' use.

For example, logic would suggest that the balance sheet should look like this (Table 2.12), with the assets clustered at the top and the liabilities (creditors over one year including long-term loans, and shareholders' funds) at the bottom.

Table 2.12   Example of a 'logical' balance sheet

		£
Fixed assets		230
Current assets, stock, debtors	140	
Less Creditors	100	
Net current assets		40
Total assets *less* Current liabilities		270
Creditors: amounts falling due after more than 1 year		100
Share capital	100	
Reserves	70	
Total shareholders' funds		170
		270

However, the Companies Act requires a balance sheet looking something like Table 2.13.

Table 2.13 Example of a balance sheet required by the Companies Act

	£	
Fixed assets		230
Current assets, stock, debtors	140	
Less Creditors	100	
Net current assets		40
Total assets *less* Current liabilities		270
Less Creditors over one year		100
		170
Share capital	100	
Reserves	70	
Total shareholders' funds		170

Here we show how the shareholders' funds alone have been used. The top portion of the balance sheet is a mishmash of long-term and short-term items and of assets and liabilities. For the purpose of analysis it makes no difference which layout you use. For management accounts it makes sense to use a layout that can be readily understood by managers!

Questions

1. Record the effects of the following events on the balance sheet, noting the changes you would make to existing figures, or by adding new items as necessary. Remember every transaction

must have at least two effects on the balance sheet. Look back at the dual aspect concept on page 19 to remind yourself how this works. After you have finished recording the events, prepare a closing balance sheet.

- Stock costing £250 was sold for £400, received in cash.
- Freehold land costing £15,000 was purchased by paying £1,500 cash and taking a 20-year mortgage for the balance.
- A company car costing £3,000 was purchased, High Finance agreeing to pay the dealer cash in 60 days.
- Stock costing £3,000 was purchased, the supplier agreeing to payment within 30 days.
- Stock costing £1,800 was sold for £2,700, the customer agreeing to pay within 120 days.

(All these transactions can be assumed to have happened over a period of a few days.)

High Finance Ltd
Balance sheet at 10 April, year _____

	£	£
Fixed assets		–
Working capital		
Current assets		
Stock	1,800	
Cash	13,300	
	15,100	
Less Current liabilities		
Overdraft	5,000	
Net current assets		10,100
Total		10,100
Financed by		
Share capital		10,000
Retained earnings (reserves)		100
		10,100

2. The following is a list of items you would normally expect to find in a profit-and-loss account. Unfortunately they are not in the right order. Rearrange them in the correct order, and so arrive at the business's net profit after tax.

	£
Purchases during the period	90,000
Miscellaneous expenses	1,900
Interest expenses	3,000
Sales	174,000
Rent from subletting part of workshop	400
Provision for income tax	3,275
Opening stock	110,000
Administration expenses	21,000
Selling expenses	7,000
Advertising expenses	2,100
Closing stock at end of the period	73,700

3

Cash flow and funds flow – where we are going

One of the characteristics that most new or small businesses have in common is a tendency to change their size and shape quickly. In the early months and years customers are few, and each new customer (or particularly big order) can mean a large percentage increase in sales. A large increase in sales in turn means an increase in raw materials and perhaps more wages and other expenses. Generally, these expenses have to be met before your customer pays up; not, however, before his order appears on your profit-and-loss account as additional income, and perhaps profit. Remember that income is realised in the profit-and-loss account when the 'goods' are dispatched and the invoice raised. But until the money comes in, the business has to find cash to meet its bills. If it cannot find the cash to meet these day-to-day bills, then it becomes 'illiquid' and very often goes bust.

Overtrading

Bankers have a name for it. They call it overtrading. Put simply, it means taking on more business than you have the cash to finance. The following simple example illustrates the problem.

A case study in overtrading (and how to avoid doing it)

The High Note Company is a new business, set up to retail music products, including sheet music, instruments and CDs/tapes. Customers will include schools, colleges and other institutions that will expect trade credit, and members of the public who will pay cash. The owner plans to put in £10,000 and he has high hopes of borrowing a further £10,000 from his bank. The premises being taken on are in good repair, but £12,500 will have to be spent on fixtures and fittings. This will leave £7,500 to meet immediate trading expenses, but customers' cash should come in quickly enough to meet day-to-day bills. The rent, rates and other basic expenses (telephone, heat, light, power and transport) should come to £27,600 over the full year. (This will include running repairs and renewals of fittings.) Apart from the owner, staff wages and bookkeeping costs will be £12,000. It is also planned to spend £250 per month on advertising. The first six months are going to be the most crucial; however, High Note's owner is confident of sales of £60,000 in that period, and the average mark-up across the product range will be 50 per cent. On this basis, the profit-and-loss account shown in Table 3.1 was prepared.

Table 3.1 Projected profit-and-loss account for High Note

High Note
Projected profit-and-loss account – six months, April–September*

	£	£
Sales		60,000
Cost of goods sold		30,000
Gross profit		30,000
Expenses†		
Rent, rates, etc	13,800	
Wages	6,000	
Advertising	1,500	21,300
Net profit before interest charges and tax		8,700

*Note that as this is a six-month period, only half the expenses are included.
†Strictly speaking, we should either depreciate or write off the fixtures and fittings. In this simplified case, this has been omitted.

This appears to be a very respectable profit, certainly enough to support a £10,000 loan, and perhaps enough to support the owner. However, this is not the whole picture. Customers will not pay on the nail; suppliers will want cash as this is a new business; wage earners and the landlord will want immediate payment. So the cash position will look more like that shown in Table 3.2.

The top of the cash-flow forecast shows the cash coming into the business each month. While High Note had a sales income in the first six months of £60,000, only £48,000 cash came in. Some customers have yet to pay up. Also the owner's start-up capital comes in, in April, along with the loan capital.

Table 3.2   Six-month cash-flow forecast for High Note

High Note
Six-month cash-flow forecast

	April £	May £	June £	July £	Aug £	Sept £	Totals for sales and purchases only £
Cash receipts in*							
Sales	4,000	5,000	5,000	7,000	12,000	15,000	48,000
Owner's capital	10,000						
Loan capital	10,000						
Total cash in	24,000	5,000	5,000	7,000	12,000	15,000	
Cash payments out							
Purchases	5,500	2,950	4,220	7,416	9,332	9,690	39,108
Rent, rates, etc	2,300	2,300	2,300	2,300	2,300	2,300	
Wages	1,000	1,000	1,000	1,000	1,000	1,000	
Advertising	250	250	250	250	250	250	
Fixtures and fittings	12,500	–	–	–	–	–	
Total cash out	21,550	6,500	7,770	10,966	12,882	13,240	
Cash balances							
Monthly cash balance	2,450	(1,500)	(2,770)	(3,966)	(882)	1,760	
Balance brought forward	–	2,450	950	(1,820)	(5,786)	(6,668)	
Balance to carry forward or Net cash flow	2,450	950	(1,820)	(5,786)	(6,668)	(4,908)	

*Value added tax is paid and collected by all businesses with a turnover greater than £51,000 per annum (2000). To keep this example simple, VAT has been ignored, but you should remember that you will probably have to show VAT separately; that is, Sales and VAT on Sales separately, and quarterly cash payments to the Customs and Excise.

The middle of the cash-flow forecast shows the cash payments out of the business. Purchases of instruments, sheet music, books, CDs and tapes make up the largest element of this; £30,000's worth of purchases are needed to support sales of £60,000 (gross margin 50 per cent), and at least one month's stock has to be available in September to meet October's demand.

So, £39,108 must be paid out to suppliers. Following this are all the other cash payments listed in the months they are to be paid.

The bottom of the cash-flow forecast shows the cash balances. The monthly cash balance shows the surplus (or deficit in brackets) for each month; the balance brought forward shows the amount brought forward from the preceding month, and the balance to carry forward shows the cumulative cash position, or net cash flow as it is usually called.

For the first two months of trading, High Note has enough cash to meet its needs. But from June to August the company needs £6,668 cash to meet current needs. By this stage most of the owner's time is probably being spent badgering good customers to pay up early, very often driving them into the arms of competitors, pleading with suppliers for credit, or, worse still, searching out inferior sources of supply. The business is now being constrained by a cash corset and the needs of the marketplace have become a low priority.

Forecasting cash needs

Fortunately, this cash-flow statement is a projection and High Note still has time to prevent such problems. From the trend of the figures it looks as though the cash deficit will be wiped out by Christmas. If this is the case perhaps an overdraft could provide an answer. However, Christmas is probably a high sales period, so the cash position might deteriorate again. As a general rule, if a business is alternating between periods of cash surplus and cash deficit, an overdraft is the answer. If there are no periods of cash surplus, then the business is under-capitalised. In other words, either the owner must put in more cash or, if the profit warrants it, more outside money can be borrowed, long term.

While High Note was a fictional example, the experience for new and small businesses is an all too common one. It is vital to forecast cash flow month by month for the year ahead. It would be prudent to look ahead for a further year or so on a quarterly basis. The ratios explained in Chapter 6, Control of working capital (or liquidity), will provide some pointers as to how the cash-flow forecast can be made. If you are asking other people to invest in your business proposition, the cash-flow forecast will be even more interesting than the projected profit. This forecast will reveal your chance of survival long enough to collect your 'profits'.

Questions

Working through the following questions will help you to consolidate your understanding of cash flow and the other two important financial statements.

1. Work out High Note's closing balance sheet at the end of September. Use the information given in the example. Remember that they will have to collect £12,000 from customers; they are carrying forward £9,108 of stock, and they have 'acquired' an overdraft of £4,908.
2. Rework the cash-flow forecast for High Note, making the following revised assumptions: first, they receive £1,000 per month more cash in from customers. Second, the fixtures and fittings cost £2,000 less, ie £10,500. Your answer should provide a pleasant surprise for High Note's owner and his bankers.
3. Check if you agree with the answer to Question 2, then recalculate the profit-and-loss-account for the six months' trading and the closing balance sheet. (Once again, ignore depreciation of fixtures and fittings.)

Funds flow

The cash-flow statement looks at the forecast movement of cash in and out of the business, but, as we already know, cash is not the only money in the business. The term 'funds' is used to mean 'cash and credit', which is nearly but not quite the same as cash. From a historical point of view, a business would want to look back at the past sources and applications of funds to help predict future funding patterns.

The funds-flow statement is prepared from the package of accounts. This is the opening and closing balance sheet, and the intervening profit-and-loss account. Look at the example on page 47, which puts these balance sheets side by side, followed by a profit-and-loss account.

Now by subtracting the opening balance sheet from the closing balance sheet and using the profit, from the profit-and-loss account we can prepare the funds-flow statement for 2001 as follows:

Sources and applications of funds statement

			£
Cash and liquid funds at start of year			(1,320)
(cash + overdraft = £8,680 + (£10,000))			
Sources of funds		£	
From trading, ie last year's profit		31,060	
before tax			
From new long-term loan		16,000	47,060
			45,740
Applications (uses of funds)		£	
Purchase of fixed assets		23,000	
Tax paid		5,920	
Increase in working capital	£		
Stock (29,300–19,840)	9,460		
Debtors (77,600–49,460)	28,140		
Creditors* (58,280–48,000)	(10,280)	27,320	
			£
			56,240
Cash and liquid funds at year end			(10,500)
(cash + overdraft = £1,500 + (£12,000))			45,740

*Creditors are people you have borrowed money from, so that has to be subtracted.

Package of accounts for funds-flow analysis at 31 December 2000 and 31 December 2001

	2000			2001
	£	£	£	£
Fixed assets		37,340		60,340
Working capital				
Current assets				
Stock	19,840		29,300	
Debtors	49,460		77,600	
Cash	8,680		1,500	
	77,980		108,400	
Less Current liabilities				
Bank overdraft	10,000		12,000	
Creditors	48,000		58,280	
Tax	5,920		9,000	
	63,920		79,280	
Net current assets		14,060		29,120
Total assets		51,400		89,460
Financed by				
Share capital		20,000		20,000
Retained earnings		11,400		33,460
Long-term loan		20,000		36,000
(at 12%)				
		51,400		89,460

Profit-and-loss account 31 December 2000–31 December 2001

	£
Sales	672,060
Gross profit	110,900
Expenses	75,520
Operating profit	35,380
Loan interest	4,320
Net profit before tax	31,060

Question

Now try and answer the following question on funds flow.

4. Look at the Parkwood and Company accounts on page 81. Calculate the funds-flow statement using that information.

Part 2

The tools of financial analysis

4 *Business controls*

An understanding of financial reports is essential to anyone who wants to control a business, but simply knowing how these reports are constructed is not enough. To be effective, the businessman must be able to analyse and interpret that financial information.

It is highly likely that a business will want to borrow money either to get started or to expand. Bankers and other sources of finance will use specialised techniques to help them decide whether or not to invest. These techniques are the same as those used by the prudent businessman. Understanding them will help you to speak the same language as the bankers.

The starting point for any useful analysis is some appreciation of what should be happening in a given situation. If, for example, you fill your car with petrol until it flows out, you expect the fuel gauge to read 'full'. If it does not you would think the gauge suspect. (If you had left someone else to fill up the car you might have other doubts as well.) This would also be true for any other car you may come across.

Business objectives

There are universal methods of measuring what is happening in a business. All businesses have two fundamental objectives in common which allows us to see how well (or otherwise) they are doing.

Making a satisfactory return on investment

The first of these objectives is to make a satisfactory return (profit) on the money invested in the business.* It is hard to think of a sound argument against this aim. To be 'satisfactory' the return must meet four criteria:

First, it must give a fair return to shareholders, bearing in mind the risk they are taking. If the venture is highly speculative and the profits are less than building society rates, your shareholders (yourself included) will not be happy.

Second, you must make enough profit to allow the company to grow. If a business wants to expand sales it will need more working capital and eventually more space or equipment. The safest and surest source of money for this is internally generated profits, retained in the business – reserves. You will remember from the balance sheet that a business has three sources of new money: share capital or the owner's money; loan capital, put up by banks, etc; and retained profits, generated by the business.

Third, the return must be good enough to attract new investors or lenders. If investors can get a greater return on their money in some other comparable business, then that is where they will put it.

Fourth, the return must provide enough reserves to keep the real capital intact. This means that you must recognise the impact inflation has on the business. A business retaining enough profits each year to meet a 5 per cent growth in assets is actually contracting by 5 per cent if inflation is running at 10 per cent.

To control the business we have to examine carefully the various factors that affect return on investment.** Shareholders' and other lenders' funds are invested in the capital, both fixed and working, of the business, so this must be the area we relate to profitability. The example in Table 4.1 shows the factors that directly influence the return on capital employed (ROCE). Capital employed = investment; remember the balance sheet must balance.

You can see that this is nothing more than a profit-and-loss account on the left and the capital employed section of the balance sheet on the right. Any change that increases net profit (eg more sales, lower expenses, less tax) but does not increase the amount of capital

---

* One of the most well-known returns on investment is the building society deposit rate. In recent years this has ranged between 3 and 8 per cent, so for every £100 invested, depositors received between £3 and £8 return, each year. Their capital, in this example £100, remained intact and secure.

**Return on investment is calculated in a number of different ways. The methods most suitable for a small business are covered in Chapter 5.

employed will increase the ROCE percentage. Any decrease in capital employed (eg lower stocks, fewer debtors) that does not lower profits will also increase ROCE. Conversely, any change that increases capital employed without increasing profits in proportion will reduce ROCE.

We shall look in detail at all the important factors that affect ROCE in Chapter 5.

Table 4.1 Factors that affect the return on capital employed (ROCE)

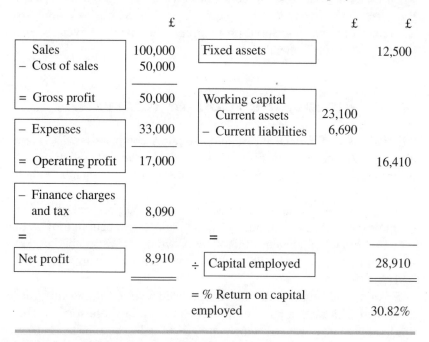

	£		£	£
Sales	100,000	Fixed assets		12,500
− Cost of sales	50,000			
= Gross profit	50,000	Working capital		
		Current assets	23,100	
− Expenses	33,000	− Current liabilities	6,690	
= Operating profit	17,000			16,410
− Finance charges and tax	8,090			
=		=		
Net profit	8,910	÷ Capital employed		28,910
		= % Return on capital employed		30.82%

Maintaining a sound financial position

As well as making a satisfactory return, investors, creditors and employees expect a business to be protected from unnecessary risks. Clearly, all businesses are exposed to market risks: competitors, new products and price changes are all part of a healthy commercial environment.

The sort of unnecessary risks that investors and lenders are particularly concerned about are high financial risks.

We have already seen how High Note (page 42) ran out of cash trying to make a very high return (87 per cent – £8,700 on £10,000 share capital). This was a financial risk decision, and whether taken or stumbled into by High Note's management, it exposed the business to the threat of liquidation.

Cash-flow problems are not the only threat to a business's financial position. Heavy borrowings can bring a big interest burden to a small business. This may be acceptable when sales and profits are good, and when times are bad shareholders can be asked to tighten their belts. Bankers, however, expect to be paid all the time. So business analysis and control are not just about profitability, but about survival and the practice of sound financial disciplines.

Ratios, the tools of analysis

All analysis of financial information requires comparisons. We have already seen that certain objectives are fundamental to all types of business. It is also true that there are three yardsticks against which business performance can be measured.

First, you can see how well you are meeting a personal goal. For example, you may want to double sales or add 25 per cent to profits. In a more formalised business this activity would be called budgeting, and comparisons would be made between actual results and the budget.

Second, you might want to see how well you are doing this year compared with last, comparing performance against a historical standard. This is the way in which growth in sales or profits is often measured. There are two main limitations to this sort of comparison. One rarely affects a small business and one affects all sizes of business.

If accounting methods change from year to year, perhaps in the way depreciation is dealt with, then you are not comparing like with like. Also the pounds in one year are not the same as the pounds in another, simply because inflation has changed them, so a 10 per cent growth in sales when inflation is running at 15 per cent represents a drop in real sales volume.

Third, you may want to see how well you are doing compared with someone else's business, perhaps a competitor, or someone in a similar line of business elsewhere. This may provide useful pointers to where improvements can be made, or to new and more profitable business opportunities. For this type of analysis you need external information. Fortunately, the UK has an unrivalled wealth of readily available financial data on companies and industries. The chief sources of this information are explained in Chapter 5.

The main way in which all these business yardsticks are established is through the use of *ratios*. A ratio is simply something expressed as a proportion of something else, and it is intended to give an appreciation of what has happened. For example, a percentage is a particular type of ratio, where events are always compared with a base of 100.

We have already seen earlier in this chapter the return on capital employed ratio, which was expressed as a percentage. In our everyday lives we apply ratios to tell us how well, or otherwise, something is performing. One measure of a car's performance is in miles per gallon (mpg). If the mpg rate drops, say, from 35 to 1 to 20 to 1, it tells us that the car is long overdue for a service – or worse. Statisticians tell us that the average number of children in a family is 1.8. That is a ratio of 1.8 children to one couple.

In the financial field the opportunity for calculating ratios is great; for useful ratios, not quite so great. Chapters 5 to 7 concentrate on explaining the key ratios for a small business. Most you can calculate yourself, some you may need your bookkeeper or accountant to organise for you. All take a little time and may cost a little money, but they do tell you a lot about what is going on. Derek Bok, a president of Harvard University, summed up this field nicely in the following quotation, 'If you think knowledge is expensive, try ignorance.'

The main value of financial analysis using ratios is that it points to questions that needs answers. A large difference between what actually happened and what standard was set suggests that something may be wrong. The tools of analysis (the ratios covered in the next three chapters) allow managers to choose from the hundreds of questions that might be asked, the handful that are really worth answering. In a small or expanding business where time is at a considerable premium, this quick pre-selection of key questions is vital.

In the examples given in the following chapters, year-end balance sheets and annual profit-and-loss accounts have been used to calculate ratios. It would be more usual and useful to use monthly accounts for internal control, but for the purposes of illustration annual figures are satisfactory.

Some problems in using ratios

Finding the information to calculate business ratios is often not the major problem. Being sure of what the ratios are really telling you almost always is.

The most common problems lie in the following four areas. (It would be very useful to read this section again, after reading the next three chapters.)

Which way is right?

There is a natural feeling with financial ratios that high figures are good ones, and that an upward trend represents the right direction. This theory is, to some extent, encouraged by the personal feeling of wealth that having a lot of cash engenders.

Unfortunately, there is not general rule on which way is right for financial ratios. In some cases a high figure is good, in others a low figure is best. Indeed, there are even circumstances in which ratios of the same value are not as good as each other.

Look at the two working capital statements in Table 4.2.

Table 4.2   Difficult comparison of ratios

	1.		2.	
Current assets	£	£	£	£
Stock	10,000		22,990	
Debtors	13,000		100	
Cash	100	23,100	10	23,100
Less Current liabilities				
Overdraft	5,000		90	
Creditors	1,690	6,690	6,600	6,690
Working capital		16,410		16,410
Current ratio*		3.4:1		3.4:1

* Current ratio = Current assets + Current liabilities. It is explained in greater detail in Chapter 6, Control of working capital (or liquidity).

The amount of working capital in each example is the same, £16,410, as are the current assets and current liabilities, at £23,100 and £6,690 respectively. It follows that any ratio using these factors would also be the same. For example, the current ratios in these two examples are both identical, 3.4:1, but in the first case there is a reasonable chance that some cash will come in from debtors, certainly enough to meet the modest creditor position. In the second example there is no possibility of useful amounts of cash coming in from trading, with debtors at only £100, while creditors at the relatively substantial figure of £6,600 will pose a real threat to financial stability. So in this case the current ratios are identical, but the situations being compared are not. In fact, as a general rule, a higher working capital ratio is regarded as a move in the wrong direction. The more money a business has tied up in working capital, the more difficult it is to make a satisfactory return on capital employed, simply because the larger the denominator, the lower the return on capital employed.

In some cases the right direction is more obvious. A high return on capital employed is usually better than a low one, but even this situation can be a danger signal, warning that higher risks are being taken. And not all high profit ratios are good: sometimes a higher profit margin can lead to reduced sales volume and so lead to a lower ROCE.

In general, business performance as measured by ratios is best thought of as lying within a range, liquidity (current ratio), for example, staying between 1.5:1 and 2.5:1. A change in either direction represents a cause for concern.

Accounting for inflation

Financial ratios all use pounds as the basis for comparison – historical pounds at that. This would not be so bad if all these pounds were from the same date in the past, but that is not so. Comparing one year with another may not be very meaningful unless we account for the change in value of the pound.

One way of overcoming this problem is to 'adjust for inflation', perhaps using an index, such as that for consumer prices. Such indices usually take 100 as their base at some time in the past, for example, 1975. Then an index value for each subsequent year is produced showing the relative movement in the item being indexed.

The two tables below show how this could be done for High Note.

Table 4.3 Comparison of unadjusted ratios

Year	Sales £	Sales growth £	Percentage growth (ie, the ratio year on year)
1	100,000	–	–
2	130,000	30,000	30
3	145,000	15,000	11.5

The unadjusted figures in Table 4.3 show a substantial growth in sales in each of the past two years.

Now if High Note's owner used a consumer price index for the appropriate time period to adjust high figures, the years could be properly compared. Let us assume that the indices for years 1, 2 and 3 were 104, 120 and 135 respectively. Year 3 is the most recent set of figures, and therefore the one we want to use as the base for comparison.

So to convert the pounds from years 1 and 2 to current pounds, we use this sum:

$$\text{Current pounds} = \frac{\text{Index for current year}}{\text{Index for historic year}} \times \text{Historic pounds}$$

For year 1   sales now become $135/104 \times £100,000 = £129,808$
2    $135/120 \times £130,000 = £146,250$
3* $135/135 \times £145,000 = £145,000$

We can now construct an adjusted table (Table 4.4), showing the real sales growth over the past three years.

Table 4.4 Comparison of adjusted ratios

Year	Adjusted sales £	Adjusted sales growth £	Adjusted growth rates %
1	129,808	–	–
2	146,250	16,442	12.7
3	145,000	–1,250	–0.9

* In other words, year 3 is virtually 'now'.

The real situation is nothing like as rosy as we first thought. The sales growth in year 2 is barely a third of the original estimate. In year 3, High Note did not grow at all – in fact it contracted slightly.

The principle of this technique can be applied to any financial ratio. The appropriate index will, to some extent, depend on the nature of the business in question. To find published data, you need to look at the *Annual Abstract of Statistics* or the *Monthly Digest Abstract of Statistics* for the retail price index.

Apples and pears

There are particular problems in trying to compare one business's ratios with another. You would not expect a Mini to be able to cover a mile as quickly as a Jaguar. A small new business can achieve quite startling sales growth ratios in the early months and years. Expanding from £10,000 sales in the first six months to £50,000 in the second would not be unusual. To expect a mature business to achieve the same growth would be unrealistic. For ICI to grow from sales of £5 billion to £25 billion would imply wiping out every other chemical company in the world. So some care must be taken to make sure that like is being compared with like, and allowances made for differing circumstances in the business being compared (or if the same business, the trading/ economic environment of the years being compared).

It is also important to check that one business's idea of an account category, say current assets, is the same as the one you want to compare it with. The concepts and principles used to prepare accounts leave some scope for differences, as Chapter 1 demonstrates.

Seasonal factors

Many of the ratios that we have looked at make use of information in the balance sheet. Balance sheets are prepared at one moment in time, and may not represent the average situation. For example, seasonal factors can cause a business's sales to be particularly high one or twice a year. A balance sheet prepared just before one of these seasonal upturns might show very high stocks, bought in specially to meet this demand. Conversely, a look at the balance sheet just after the upturn might show very high cash and low stocks. If either of those stock figures were to be treated as an average it would give a false picture.

Ratios in forecasting

Ratios have another valuable use – they can be an aid to making future financial projections. For example, if you believe it prudent to hold the equivalent of a month's sales in stock, once you have made the sales forecast for future years, the projections for stock in the balance sheet follow automatically.

Questions

1. What are the two fundamental objectives that every business has in common?
2. Look back to the example of factors that can affect the return on capital employed on page 53. Assume that the gross profit will remain at a constant £50,000, whatever changes you decide to make. Recommend four changes that would increase ROCE.
3. What yardsticks could you use to measure your business's performance?
4. High Note's sales figures for the first three years have been confirmed as £100,000, £130,000 and £160,000 respectively. You also know that the consumer index for each year was 106, 124 and 140. Calculate the unadjusted sales-growth ratios. Compare them with the ratios you get once you have accounted for inflation.

5 Measures of profitability

There are two main ways to measure a business's profitability. They are both important, but they reveal different things about the performance and perhaps even the strategy of the business. To know and understand what is happening you need information in both areas: return on capital employed and profit margins.

Return on capital employed (ROCE)

The financial resources employed in a business are called *capital*. We have already seen that capital can come into a business from a number of different sources. These sources have one thing in common: they all want a return – a percentage interest – on the money they invest.

There are a number of ways in which return on capital can be measured, but for a small business two are particularly important.

The ROCE ratio is calculated by expressing the profit before long-term loan interest and tax as a proportion of the total capital employed. So if you look at the High Note profit-and-loss account on page 68 you can see that for year 1 the profit before tax is £14,850. To this we have to add the loan interest of £1,250. If we did not do this we would be double-counting our cost of loan capital by expecting a return on a loan which had already paid interest. This makes the profit figure £16,100. We also ignore tax charges, not because they are unimportant or insignificant, but simply because the level of tax is largely outside the control of the business, and it is the business's performance we are trying to measure.

Now look at the balance sheet. The capital employed is the sum of the owner's capital, the profit retained and the long-term loan, in this case £28,910 (£10,000 + £8,910 + £10,000).

So the ROCE ratio for the first year is:

$$\frac{£16,100}{£28,910} = 0.56, \text{ which expressed as percentage} = 56\%$$

The great strength of this ratio lies in the overall view it takes of the financial health of the whole business. If you look at the same ratio for the second year, you will see a small change. The ratio gives no clue as to why this has happened – it simply provides the starting point for an analysis of business performance, and an overall yardstick with which to compare absolute performance.

A banker might look to this ratio to see if the business could support more long-term borrowing (not in isolation, of course).

Return on shareholders' capital (ROSC)

The second way a small business would calculate a return on capital is by looking at the profit available for shareholders. This is not the money actually paid out, for example, as dividends, but is a measure of the increase in 'worth' of the funds invested by shareholders.

In this case the net profit after tax is divided by the owner's capital plus the retained profits (which, although not distributed, belong to the shareholders).

So in our example this would be the sum:

$$\frac{£8,910}{£18,910} = 0.47, \text{ which expressed as a percentage} = 47\%$$

And for the second year this ratio would be 41 per cent.

If someone was considering investing in shares in this business, then this ratio would be of particular interest to them.

Once again the difference in the ratios is clear, but the reasons for it are not. This is only the starting point for a more detailed analysis.

Gearing and its effects on ROSC

All businesses have access to two fundamentally different sorts of money. *Equity*, or owner's capital, including retained earnings, is money that is not a risk to the business. If no profits are made, then the owner and other shareholders simply do not get dividends. They may not be pleased, but they cannot usually sue.

Debt capital is money borrowed by the business from outside sources; it puts the business at financial risk and is also risky for the lenders. In return for taking that risk they expect an interest payment every year, irrespective of the performance of the business.

High gearing is the name given when a business has a high proportion of outside money to inside money. High gearing has considerable attractions to a business that wants to make high returns on shareholders' capital, as Table 5.1 shows.

Table 5.1 The effect of gearing on ROSC

	No gearing –	Average gearing 1:1	High gearing 2:1	Very high gearing 3:1
Capital structure	£	£	£	£
Share capital	60,000	30,000	20,000	15,000
Loan capital (at 12%)	–	30,000	40,000	45,000
Total capital	60,000	60,000	60,000	60,000
Profits				
Operating profit	10,000	10,000	10,000	10,000
Less interest on loan	None	3,600	4,800	5,400
Net profit	10,000	6,400	5,200	4,600
Return on share capital =	$\dfrac{10,000}{60,000}$	$\dfrac{6,400}{30,000}$	$\dfrac{5,200}{20,000}$	$\dfrac{4,600}{15,000}$
=	16.6%	21.3%	26%	30.7%
Times interest earned =	N/A	$\dfrac{10,000}{3,600}$	$\dfrac{10,000}{4,800}$	$\dfrac{10,000}{5,400}$
=	N/A	2.8X*	2.1X	1.8X

*X is a convention for 'times'.

In this example the business is assumed to need £60,000 capital to generate £10,000 operating profits. Four different capital structures are considered. They range from all share capital (no gearing) at one end to nearly all loan capital at the other. The loan capital has to be 'serviced', that is, interest of 12 per cent has to be paid. The loan itself can be relatively indefinitive, simply being replaced by another one at market interest rates when the first loan expires.

Following the tables through you can see that ROSC grows from 16.6 to 30.7 per cent by virtue of the changed gearing. If the interest on the loan were lower, the ROSC would be even more improved by high gearing, and the higher the interest, the lower the relative improvement in ROSC. So in times of low interest, businesses tend to go for increased borrowings rather than raising more equity, that is money from shareholders.

At first sight this looks like a perpetual profit-growth machine. Naturally owners would rather have someone else 'lend' them the money for their business than put it in themselves, if they could increase the return on their investment. The problem comes if the business does not produce £10,000 operating profits. Very often, in a small business, a drop in sales of 20 per cent means profits are halved. If profits were halved in this example, the business could not meet the interest payments on its loan. That would make the business insolvent, and so not in a 'sound financial position'; in other words, failing to meet one of the two primary business objectives.

Bankers tend to favour 1:1 gearing as the maximum for a small business, although they have been known to go much higher. (A glance at the Laker accounts will show just how far the equation can be taken, with £200 million plus of loans for a £1 million or so equity.)

As well as looking at the gearing, lenders will study the business's capacity to pay interest. They do this by using another ratio called 'times interest earned'.

This is calculated by dividing the operating profit by the loan interest. It shows how many times the loan interest is covered, and gives the lender some idea of the safety margin. The ratio for this example is given at the end of Table 5.1. Once again rules are hard to make, but much less than 3X interest earned is unlikely to give lenders confidence.

Profit margins

Any analysis of a business must consider the current level of sales activity. If you look at High Note's profit-and-loss accounts (Table 5.3 on page 68), you will see that materials consumed in sales have jumped from £30,000 to £43,000, a rise of 43 per cent. However, a quick look at the change in sales activity will show that the situation is nothing like so dramatic. Materials as a proportion of sales have risen from 30 to 33 per cent (£30,000/100,000 = 30% and 43,000/130,000 = 33%). Obviously, the more you sell, the more you must make.

To understand why there have been changes in the level of return on capital employed, we have to relate both profit and capital to sales activity. The ROCE equation can be expanded to look like this:

$$\frac{\text{Profit}}{\text{Capital}} = \frac{\text{Profit}}{\text{Sales}} \times \frac{\text{Sales}}{\text{Capital}}$$

This gives us two separate strands to examine, the profit strand and the capital strand. The first of these is usually called profit margins. The capital strand will be looked at in the next two chapters.

When we examine profit margins, all costs, expenses and the different types of profit are expressed as a percentage of sales. This ratio makes comparisons both possible and realistic.

The analysis of High Note's profit-and-loss account displayed in Table 5.2 shows changes and possible causes.

Table 5.2 An analysis of High Note's profit-and-loss account

Area	*Change*	*Some possible causes*
Material cost of sales	Up from 30% to 33%	(a) Higher prices paid (b) Change in product mix (c) Increased waste
Labour cost of sales	Down from 20% to 19%	(a) Reduction in wage rates (b) Increase in work rate (c) Change in product mix
Gross profit	Down from 50% to 48%	(a) 3% increase in materials (b) 1% increase in labour = net 2% decline in gross margin
Operating or trading profit	Up from 17% to 18.5%	A 3.5% improvement in expense ratios offset by a 2% decline in gross margin = net 1.5% improvement in trading profit.
Net profit before tax	Up from 14.8% to 16.9%	Interest charges down from 2.1% of sales to 1.6% Means another 0.5% increase in net profit + 1.5% net increase in trading profit = 2%.

Had we simply looked at the net profit margin, we would have seen a satisfactory increase, from 8.9 to 10.1 per cent. It was only by looking at each area in turn, the components of gross profit, operating or trading profit and net profit, that a useful analysis could be made. High Note's owner now has a small number of specific questions to ask in the search for reasons for changes in performance.

To summarise, the ratios of profitability that allow attention to be focused on specific areas are:

Gross profit percentage

This is deducting the cost of sales from the sales, and expressing the result as a percentage of sales.

In the High Note example for year 1, this is £100,000 (sales) − £50,000 (cost of sales) = £50,000 (gross profit); then £50,000 (gross profit) + £100,000 (sales) = 50 per cent.

This ratio gives an indication of relative manufacturing efficiency.

Operating or trading profit percentage

This is calculated by deducting expenses from the gross profit, to arrive at the operating profit. This figure is then divided by sales and expressed as a percentage. For High Note in year 1, this is £50,000 (gross profit) − £33,000 (expenses) = £17,000 (operating profit); then £17,000 (operating profit) + £100,000 (sales) = 17 per cent.

Net profit before tax percentage

In this case finance charges are deducted from operating profits to arrive at net profit before tax. This is then expressed as a percentage of sales.

For High Note in year 1, this is £17,000 (trading profit) − £2,150 (interest charge) = £14,850 (net profit before tax) = 14.85 per cent.

Table 5.3 High Note's financial statements

Profit-and-loss account for years 1 and 2

	£	£	%	£	£	%
Sales		100,000	100		130,000	100
Cost of sales						
Materials	30,000		30	43,000		33
Labour	20,000	50,000	20	25,000	68,000	19
Gross profit		50,000	50		62,000	48
Expenses						
Rent, rates, etc	18,000			20,000		
Wages	12,000			13,000		
Advertising	3,000			3,000		
Expenses		33,000		2,000	38,000	
Operating or trading profit		17,000	17		24,000	18.5
Deduct interest on:						
Overdraft	900					
Loan	1,250	2,150		1,250	2,050	
Net profit before tax		14,850	14.8		21,950	16.9
Tax paid at 40%*		5,940			8,780	
Net profit after tax		8,910	8.9		13,170	10.1

Balance sheet for year-ends 1 and 2

	£	£	£	£	£	£
Fixed assets						
Furniture and fixtures			12,500			28,110
Working capital						
Current assets						
Stock	10,000			12,000		
Debtors	13,000			13,000		
Cash	100	23,100		500	25,500	

*Business tax rates are usually changed each year in the budget. In 2000, a sole trader would be taxed at the 40 per cent rate by the time his or her profits had reached about £30,000, taking allowances into account.

A limited company wouldn't start paying higher rates of tax until its profits were £300,000.

Less Current liabilities				
Overdraft	5,000		6,000	
Creditors	1,690	6,690	5,500	11,500
Net current assets		16,410		14,000
Capital employed		28,910		42,110
Financed by				
Owner's capital	10,000		18,940	
Profit retained	8,910	18,910	13,170	32,110
Long-term loan		10,000		10,000
Total		28,910		42,110

Calculating tax due

The more successful a small business is, the greater its exposure to tax liabilities. Its exact tax position will depend on the legal nature of the business. A limited company is subject to corporation tax at a set rate announced each year by the Government. If the business is not a limited company, its proprietor is likely to be subject to income tax and to tax rates applying to the general public. Simply monitoring pre-tax ratios provides satisfactory measures of trading performance, but this is not enough. The owner/manager will be concerned with the net profit *after tax*, as this is the money that is available to help the business to grow or to overcome unforeseen problems.

Managing the tax position is one area where professional advice is essential. This is very important, as tax rules can change every year. Good advice can help to reduce the overall tax bill and so increase the value of profits to the business.

Sole traders and partnerships are treated differently to limited companies for tax purposes, so we will look at each in turn.

Sole traders and partnerships

Partnerships are treated as a collection of sole traders for tax purposes, and each partner's share of that collective liability has to be worked out. Sole (self-employed) traders have all their income from every source brought together and taxed as one entity. In the UK, the taxes that need to be calculated are:

- income tax, paid on profits;
- Class 4 National Insurance, paid on profits;
- Capital Gains Tax, paid on the disposal of fixed assets at a profit, or when the business is sold;
- inheritance tax, paid on death or when certain gifts are made.

Neither of the last two taxes are likely to occur on a regular basis, so we will not be dealing with them. When those taxes do come into play, the sums involved are likely to be significant and professional advice should be taken from the outset.

Income tax

The profit-and-loss account structure that we looked at earlier, whilst more than adequate for the purpose of running a business, is not quite sufficient for working out the likely amount of tax due. Some perfectly proper expenses that we need to account for in deciding how well (or badly) a business is performing are not allowed for tax purposes. For example, entertainment costs would appear in the management accounts, but the cost would not be allowed for tax purposes.

The rate of depreciation, for example, is a matter for each businessperson to decide for him- or herself. In the management accounts you can decide, for example, to depreciate an asset over one year or five years. The nominal effect on profits can be significant.

Certain business expenses are disallowed, partially disallowed or allowed for, but in a different way. The same methods are used by tax authorities throughout the world. After you have produced your management accounts showing what you understand to be the income and expenditure for the period to be, and have compiled a record of assets bought, a process known as a 'profit computation' has to be carried out. This adjusts that profit figure to meet the tax authorities' needs. Unsurprisingly, this will almost inevitably be a higher figure, and so a higher tax liability, than the one that you will have arrived at in your management accounts.

In the computation, some expenses are disallowed. These include depreciation, which has been replaced by capital allowances. Capital allowances are an incentive offered by governments to encourage investment in new equipment and technology. The rate is changed in the annual budget to reflect the foibles of the government of the day.

In this example, we have assumed the '*writing-down allowance*' (as it is commonly known) to be 25 per cent. However, in the first year, as an incentive to invest, the rate has been set at 40 per cent (it has been as high as 100 per cent). Any private element of expenses charged in the accounts is added back. Whilst you may dispute that you use your car for any purpose other than for business, as you have a second car, in practice it will be easier to conform to the 'norms' that require you to admit a certain percentage (in this example, 25 per cent) is for private use.

The changes that have to be made to the management accounts to arrive at the profit for tax purposes can have a significant effect on the end result. You will need to ensure that any expense that may have seemed reasonable in the management accounts meets the more stringent requirements of the tax authorities. You are generally allowed to set an expense against your income if it is:

- incurred wholly and exclusively for the purposes of trade;
- properly charged against income (not, for example, purchase of a property lease, which is capital);
- not specifically disallowed by statute (for example, you cannot set entertainment of customers against your tax, although it is a perfectly legitimate accounting expense).

Net taxable profit

Under the self-assessment tax system in the UK, the basis of the period of a year of assessment is the accounting year ending within that tax year. So if you made up your accounts to 31 December, the basis period for income tax year 2002/2003 would be 6 April 2002 to 5 April 2003. There are special rules that apply for the first year and the last year of trading that should ensure tax is charged fairly.

If your turnover is low – currently in the UK, less than £15,000 per year – you can put in a three-line account: sales, expenses and profit. If it is over the current low figure, you have to summarise your accounts to show turnover, gross profit and expenses by main heading.

You will have a personal allowance (the current threshold below which you don't pay tax). That amount is deducted from the profit figure. Then a figure is added for Class 4 National Insurance based on taxable profits that lie within a certain band. In the UK, that band is currently between about £8,000 and £26,000 and the tax rate is 6 per cent. This is paid in addition to the flat rate Class 2 contributions of about £7 per week.

All these rates and amounts are constantly changing, but the broad principles remain.

Company taxation

Companies have a separate legal identity from those who work for them, whether or not they are shareholding directors. Everyone working for the business is taxed as an employee. UK companies are responsible for collecting tax and passing it to the tax authorities through the PAYE (pay as you earn) system.

Directors' pay is a business expense, just as with any other wage, and is deducted from the company's revenue when calculating its taxable profits.

Companies in the UK pay tax in three main ways:

1. On the company's profits for the year, as calculated in the tax-adjusted profits. This is called '*corporation tax*'. The rate of corporation tax in the UK, and in many other countries, depends on the amount of profit made. If the profit is less than £300,000, the small companies rate of 20 per cent applies. If the profit is above £1.5 million, the full rate of 30 per cent is charged. For figures between, a taper applies. All these figures are subject to annual review in the budget. Corporation tax is payable nine months after the end of the accounting period.

2. On the distribution of profit to the shareholders in the dividend payment. This gives the appearance of taxing the same profit twice, but through a process of 'tax credits', this double taxation doesn't generally occur. When a shareholder gets a dividend from a company, it comes with a tax credit attached. This means that any shareholder on the basic rate of tax won't have to pay any further tax. Higher-rate tax payers, however, have a further amount of tax to pay.

3. On capital gains. If an asset – say, a business property – is sold at a profit, then the company will have made a capital gain. This

gain will be taxed along the general lines of corporation tax, but with lower rates applying to smaller companies.

As tax is a business expense for a company, an allowance for tax must be included in the accounts. When it's paid it will appear in the profit-and-loss account. Before it is paid we 'accrue' for it by showing it as a creditor in the balance sheet (an accrual is the process of managing a business event that is not documented). Generally, people send companies bills for all services rendered, so that is the 'document' in the company accounts. But where no document exists – as with tax due – yet it is recognised that the business owes the money, it is accrued for.

Which structure is best?

The most important rule is: never let the 'tax tail wag the business dog'. Tax is just one aspect of business life. If you want to keep your business's finances private, then the public filing of accounts required of companies is not for you. On the other hand, if you feel that you want to protect your private assets from creditors if things go wrong, then being a sole trader or partner is probably not the best route to take.

Company profits and losses are locked into the company, so if you have several lines of business using different trading entities you cannot easily offset losses in one area against profits in another. But as sole traders are treated as one entity for all their sources of income, there is more scope for netting off gains and losses. Some points to bear in mind here are:

- If your profits are likely to be small, say below £50,000, for some time, then from a purely tax point of view you may pay less as a sole trader. This is because, as an individual, you get a tax-free allowance – your first few thousand pounds of income are not taxable. This amount varies according to personal circumstances – whether you are married or single, for example – and can be changed in the budget each year.
- If you expect to be making higher rates of profit, say above £50,000, and want to reinvest a large portion of those profits back into your business, then you could be better off forming a company, as companies don't start paying higher rates of tax

until their profits are £300,000. Even then, companies don't pay the 40 per cent tax rate that a sole trader would if he or she were to make a profit above £30,000, taking allowances into account. So, a company making £300,000 taxable profits could have £54,000 more profit to reinvest in financing future outgoings than a sole trader in the same line of work (£240,000–£186,000).

- Non-salary benefits favour the sole trader. It is generally possible to get tax relief on the business element of costs that are only partly business related, such a running a vehicle. The director of a company would be taxed on the value of the vehicle's list price and would not be allowed travel to and from work as a business expense.

Minimising taxes

There is no need to pay more tax than you have to. Whilst staying within the law by a safe margin, you should explore ways to *avoid* as oppose to *evade* tax liability. This is a complex area and one subject to frequent change. The tax authorities constantly try to close loopholes in the tax system, whilst highly paid tax accountants and lawyers try even harder to find new ways around the rules. These are some of the areas to keep in mind when assessing your tax liability:

- Make sure you have included all allowable business expenses, especially if you have recently set up a business, as you may not be fully aware of all the expenses that can be claimed. For example, whilst entertaining clients is not an allowable business expense, the cost of your meals may well be allowable if you are away from home and staying overnight.
- If you have made losses in any tax period, these may, under certain circumstances, be carried forward to offset future taxable profits or backwards against past profits.
- Capital Gains Tax can be deferred if another asset is to be bought with the proceeds. This is known as *rollover relief* and it can normally be used up to three years after the taxable event.
- Pension contributions will reduce your taxable profits. You may even be able to set up a pension scheme that allows you to have

some say over how those funds are used. For example, your pension fund could be used to finance your business premises. The pension fund would, in effect, become your landlord. The company then pays rent, an allowable business expense, into your pension fund, which is growing tax free.

- If you do intend to buy capital assets for your business, bring forward your spending plans to maximise the use of the writing-down allowance.
- Identify non-cash benefits that you and others working for you could take instead of taxable salary. For employees, a share-option scheme may achieve the same, or better, level of reward with less tax payable.
- Examine the pros and cons of taking your money out of a limited company by dividends or salary. These are taxed differently and may provide scope for tax reduction.
- If your spouse has no other income from employment, they could earn a sum equivalent to their annual tax-free allowance (currently about £4,000) by working for your business.
- Have you any pre-trading expenses incurred at any stage over the seven years before you started up the business? They can probably be treated as if they had been incurred after trading started. Such items may include the cost of carrying out market research, designing and testing your product or service, capital items such as a computer bought before you started trading, which was then brought into the assets of your business.
- Have you bought any business assets on hire purchase? You may be able to treat the full purchase price in your capital allowances calculation.

This is an indicative rather than a comprehensive list of areas to explore. Tax is a field in which timely professional advice can produce substantial benefits in the form of lower tax bills.

Value added tax (VAT)

VAT is a tax on consumer spending. It is a European tax system, although most countries have significant variations in VAT rates, starting thresholds and in the schemes themselves. It effectively requires every business over a certain size to become a tax collector. There is no reward for carrying out this task, but there are penalties for making mistakes or for making late VAT returns.

VAT is complicated tax. Essentially, you must register if your taxable turnover (ie sales, not profit) exceeds £51,000 in any 12-month period, or if it looks as though it might reasonably be expected to do so. This rate is reviewed each year in the budget and is frequently changed. The UK is significantly out of line with many other countries in Europe, where VAT entry rates are much lower. The general rule is that all supplies of goods and services are taxable at the standard rate – 17.5 per cent – unless they are specifically stated by the law to be zero-rated or exempt. When deciding whether your turnover exceeds the limit you have to include zero-rated sales (things like most foods, books and children's clothing) as they are *technically* taxable – however, their rate of tax is 0 per cent. You leave out exempt items. There are three free booklets issued by Customs and Excise: a simple introductory booklet called *Should You be Registered for VAT?* and two more detailed booklets called *General Guide* and *Scope and Coverage*. If in doubt (the language is not easy to understand), ask your accountant or the local branch of Customs and Excise – after all, they would rather help you to get it right in the first place than have to sort it out later when you make a mess of it.

Each quarter, you will have to complete a return, which shows your purchases and the VAT you paid on them, and your sales and the VAT you collected on them. The VAT taxes paid and collected are offset against one another and the balance is sent to Customs and Excise. If you have paid more VAT in any one quarter than you have collected, you will get a refund. For this reason, it sometimes pays to register even if you don't have to – if you are selling mostly zero-rated items for example. Also, being registered for VAT may make your business appear more professional to your potential customers.

VAT records

The bookkeeping system that we started out with may need to be extended to accommodate VAT records. So the analysed cash book, if we are using a simple system, may look like Table 5.4 opposite:

Table 5.4 Value Added Tax bookkeeping records, payments

| Payments | | | | | | | | Analysis | | |
Date	Name	Details	Reference number	Net amount (£)	VAT at 17.5% (£)	Gross amount (£)	Stocks	Vehicles	Telephone
4 June	Gibbs	Stock purchase	001	263.83	46.17	310.00	263.83		
8 June	Gibbs	Stock purchase	002	110.64	19.36	130.00	110.64		
12 June	ABC Telecoms	Telephone charges	003	47.00	8.23	55.23			47.00
18 June	Colt Rentals	Vehicle hire	004	74.26	13.00	87.26		74.26	
22 June	VV Mobiles	Mobile phone	005	45.31	7.93	53.24			45.31
27 June	Gibbs	Stock purchase	006	30.88	5.40	36.28	30.88		
Totals				**571.92**	**100.09**	**672.01**	**405.35**	**74.26**	**92.31**

You can see that the single figure for the amount paid used in the pre-VAT registration bookkeeping system has been replaced by three columns. One shows the amount before VAT is charged, then the amount of the VAT followed by the gross amount including VAT. The analysis columns contain the net amounts. You can cross-check the arithmetic by totalling the three columns of analysis and confirming that they add up to the total of the net amount; in this example, £571.92.

The same layout can be used for bookkeeping records of receipts, with or without the analysis.

Doing the sum

Calculating the VAT of any transaction can be a confusing sum. These simple rules will help you to get it right every time. Take the gross amount of any sum (the total, including any VAT) and divide it into 117.5 parts if the VAT rate is 17.5 per cent (if the VAT rate is not 17.5 per cent, use the figure that corresponds to the VAT rate plus 100). All this means is that we are saying that the bill we have received is 100 per cent of the net bill with another 17.5 per cent added on top.

Then we can take a 117.5th part of the bill and multiply it by 100 to get the pre-VAT total and multiply by 17.5 to arrive at the VAT element of the bill (see Figure 5.1).

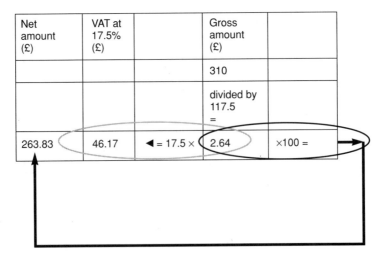

Figure 5.1   Calculating VAT sums

Doing the VAT return

This has to be where a computer-based bookkeeping system wins hands down. VAT returns (or 'sales tax returns' in the US) can be automatically generated by an accounting package. When using such a package, all you have to do is enter the current VAT rate. If you take Web-enabled software updates, you may not even have to do this. Basically, the VAT inspectors are interested in five figures (see Figure 5.2):

● how much VAT you have collected on their behalf on the goods and services you have sold;
● how much VAT has been collected from you by those who have sold you goods and services;

The difference between those two sums is, if positive, the VAT due to be paid, or, if negative, the amount of VAT to be reclaimed. For businesses VAT is a zero sum game, it's the end consumer who picks up the tab.

The final two numbers are a check on the reasonableness of the whole sum. Here you must show the value of your sales and purchases net of VAT for the period in question. The VAT return has to be signed by the person registered for VAT. It's important to remember that a named person is responsible for VAT, as a limited company is treated as a 'person' in this instance. Not only does it act as an unpaid tax collector but there are penalties for filing a return late or incorrectly. VAT records have to be kept for six years and periodically you can expect a visit from a VAT inspector.

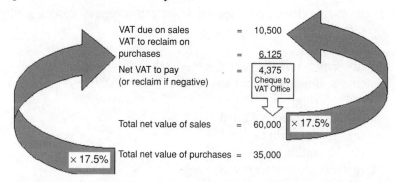

Figure 5.2   The essence of the VAT return

Cash accounting

If your business has a turnover greater than £350,000 a year, then you have no option but to account for VAT in the usual way. That means that income will be recognised when you raise an invoice rather than when you get paid. Unfortunately, the VAT will have to be paid when it is due, whether you have been paid or not. If your turnover is less than £350,000, then you can elect to pay VAT on a cash basis. This means you are not liable for the VAT until your customers pay up. But it also means you can't reclaim VAT on any purchases until you actually pay for them. In the early years of running a business, when cash flow is usually tight, or when you have a small number of customers who buy a large proportion of your output on credit, this might be an option worth pursuing.

Other matters

We have only sketched an outline of VAT here. There are a number of special schemes for retailers, adjustments to be made for any private usage, different ways of handling certain second-hand goods and scale charges to be applied to the use of motor vehicles. So, it is advisable to get the free booklets on offer from the VAT authorities and to take professional advice if you have any doubts.

Question

1. From the Parkwood accounts set out overleaf calculate the following ratios for each year:

   (a) return on total capital employed;
   (b) return on shareholders' capital (after tax);
   (c) gearing;
   (d) times interest earned;
   (e) gross profit;
   (f) operating profit
   (g) net profit after tax.

Parkwood & Co balance sheet at 20 January 2000 and 2001 respectively

	£	2000 £	£	2001 £
Fixed assets		18,670		30,170
Working capital				
Current assets				
Stock	9,920		14,650	
Debtors	24,730		38,800	
Cash	4,340		750	
	38,990		54,200	
Less Current liabilities				
Bank overdraft	5,000		6,000	
Creditors	24,000		29,140	
Tax	2,960		4,500	
	31,960		39,640	
Net current assets		7,030		14,560
Total assets		25,700		44,730
Financed by				
Share capital		10,000		10,000
Retained earnings		5,700		16,730
Long-term loan		10,000		18,000
(at 12%)				
		25,700		44,730

Profit-and-loss account

	1999 £	2000 £
Sales	249,340	336,030
Cost of goods sold	209,450	280,580
Gross profit	39,890	55,450
Expenses		
Sales and marketing	10,000	15,000
Administration	10,000	20,000
General	6,668	2,760
Total expenses	26,668	37,760
Operating profit	13,222	17,690
Loan interest	1,200	2,160
Net profit before tax	12,022	15,530
Tax due on profits	4,809	4,500
Net profit after tax	7,213	11,030

6 Control of working capital (or liquidity)

The capital strand of the return on capital employed (ROCE) calculation has two main branches of its own.

$$\frac{\text{Sales}}{\text{Capital}} \text{ (ROCE)} = \frac{\text{Sales}}{\text{Fixed assets and Working capital}}$$

The more dynamic of these is working capital, the day-to-day money used to finance the working of the business. It is important to monitor the relationship between sales and the various elements of working capital, to see how effectively that capital is being used. But as the working capital is the difference between current assets and current liabilities, it is also important to monitor their relationship, both in total and in their component parts.

This area is very often referred to as liquidity, or the business's ability to meet its current liabilities as they fall due. The most important ratios in this area are: the current ratio, the quick ratio or acid test, credit control, stock control and cash control.

The current ratio

A business's ability to meets its immediate liabilities can be estimated by relating its current assets to its current liabilities. If for any reason current liabilities cannot be met, then the business is being exposed to an unacceptable level of financial risk. Suppliers may stop supplying or could even petition for bankruptcy if they are kept waiting too long for payments.

In our accounts for High Note (on page 68) the first year' picture on the balance sheet shows £23,100 current assets to £6,690 current liabilities.

$$\text{Current ratio} \; = \; \frac{\text{Current assets}}{\text{Current liabilities}}$$

$$\text{Therefore, High Note's current ratio} \; = \; \frac{23,100}{6,690} = 3.4$$

This shows current liabilities to be covered 3.4 times, and the ratio is usually expressed in the form of 3.4:1.

In the second year this has come down to 2.2:1.

At first glance this figure may look worse than the first year's position. Certainly, current liabilities have grown faster than current assets, but up to a point this is a desirable state of affairs, because it means the business is having to find less money to finance working capital.

There is really only one rule about how high (or low) the current ratio should be. It should be as close to 1:1 as the safe conduct of the business will allow. This will not be the same for every type of business.

A shop buying in finished goods on credit and selling them for cash could run safely at 1.3:1. A manufacturer, with raw materials to store and customers to finance, may need over 2:1. This is because the period between paying cash out for raw materials and receiving cash in from customers is longer in a manufacturing business than in a retail business.

It is a bit like the oil dipstick on a car. There is a band within which the oil level should be. Levels above or below that band pose different problems. So for most businesses, less than 1.2:1 would probably be cutting things a bit fine. Over 1.8:1 would mean too much cash was being tied up in such items as stock and debtors.

An unnecessarily high amount of working capital makes it harder for a business to make a good ROCE because it makes the bottom half of the sum bigger.* Too low a working capital, below 1:1 for example, exposes the business to unacceptable financial risks, eg foreclosure by banks or creditors.

The quick ratio or acid test

The quick ratio is really a belt and braces figure. In this, only assets that can be realised quickly, such as debtors and cash in hand, are related to current liabilities.

$$\text{Quick ratio} \quad = \quad \frac{\text{Cash} + \text{Debtors}}{\text{Current liabilities}}$$

For our example, looking at year one only, we would exclude the £10,000 stock because, before it can be realised, we would need to find customers to sell to and collect in the cash. All this might take several months. High Note's quick ratio would be 13,100 (cash + debtors) ÷ 6,690 (current liabilities): a perhaps too respectable 1.9:1. In the second year this has dropped to 1.2:1 (13,500 ÷ 11,500).

Once again general rules are very difficult to make, but a ratio of 0.8:1 would be acceptable for most types of business.

Credit control

Any small business selling on credit knows just how quickly customers can eat into their cash. This is particularly true if the customers are big companies. Surprisingly enough, bad debts (those that are never paid) are rarely as serious a problem as slow payers. Many companies think nothing of taking three months' credit, and it is important to remember that even if your terms are 30 days it will be nearer 45 days *on average* before you are paid. This to some extent depends on how frequently invoices are sent out. Assuming they do not go out each day – and

---

*Remember ROCE = Profit ÷ Total capital employed, and Total capital = Fixed assets + Working capital.

perhaps more importantly, your customer *does* batch his or her bills for payment monthly – then that is how things will work out.

There are two techniques for monitoring debtors. The first is to prepare a schedule by 'age' of debtor. Table 6.1 gives some idea of how this might be done.

Table 6.1 High Note's debtors schedule – end of year 1

	2 months (or less) £	3 months £	4 months £	Over 4 months £	Total £
Brown & Co	1,000				
Jenkins & Son	1,000				
Andersons		3,000			
Smithers		2,500			
Thomkinsons			500		
Henry's			2,500		
Smart Inc				2,500	
	2,000	5,500	3,000	2,500	13,000

This method has the greater merit of focusing attention clearly on specific problem accounts. It may seem like hard work, but once you have got the system going it will pay dividends.

The second technique for monitoring debtors is using the ratio *average collection period*.

This ratio is calculated by expressing debtors as a proportion of credit sales, and then relating that to the days in the period in question.

$$\text{Average collection period} = \frac{\text{Debtors}}{\text{Sales}} \times 365$$

Let us suppose that all High Note's sales are on credit and the periods in question are both 365-day years (ie no leap years). Then in year 1 the average collection period would be:

$$\frac{\text{£13,000 Debtors}}{\text{£100,000 Sales}} \times 365 \text{ (days in period)} = 47 \text{ days}$$

In year 2 the collection period is:

$$\frac{\text{£13,000 Debtors}}{\text{£130,000 Sales}} \times 365 \text{ (days in period)} = 36 \text{ days}$$

So in the second year High Note are collecting their cash from debtors 11 days sooner than in the first year. This is obviously a better position to be in, making their relative amount of debtors lower than in year 1. It is not making the absolute amount of debtors lower, and this illustrates another great strength of using ratios to monitor performance. High Note's sales have grown by 30 per cent from £100,000 to £130,000, and their debtors have remained at £13,000.

At first glance then, their debtors are the same, neither better nor worse. But when you relate those debtors to the increased levels of sales, as this ratio does, then you can see that the position has improved.

This is a good control ratio, which has the great merit of being quickly translatable into a figure any businessman can understand, showing how much it is costing to give credit.

If, for example, High Note is paying 12 per cent for an overdraft, then giving £13,000 credit for 36 days will cost £153.86 ((12% × £13,000 × 36) ÷ 365).

Average days' credit taken

Of course, the credit world is not all one sided. Once a small business has established itself, it too will be taking credit. You can usually rely on your suppliers to keep you informed on your indebtedness – but only on an individual basis. It would be prudent to calculate how many days' credit, on average, are being taken from suppliers: a very similar sum to the average collection period. The ratio is as follows:

$$\text{Average collection period} = \frac{\text{Creditors}}{\text{Purchases}} \times 365$$

For High Note, in year 1 this sum would be:

$$\frac{\text{£1,690 Creditors}}{\text{*£30,000 Purchases}} \times 365 \text{ (days in period)} = 21 \text{ days}$$

In year 2 this ratio would be:

$$\frac{\text{£5,500 Creditors}}{\text{£43,000 Purchases}} \times 365 \text{ (days in period)} = 47 \text{ days}$$

The difference in these ratios probably reflects High Note's greater creditworthiness in year 2. The longer the credit period you can take from your suppliers the better, provided that you still meet their terms of trade. They may, however, put you to the bottom of the list when supplies get scarce, or give you up altogether when they find a 'better' customer.

More creditor controls

There are two other useful techniques to help the owner-manager keep track of these events. One is simply to relate days' credit given to days' credit taken. If they balance out, then you are about even in the credit game.

In year 1, High Note gave 47 days' credit to their customers and took only 21 days from their suppliers, so they were a loser. In the second year they got ahead, giving only 36 days while taking 47.

The other technique is to 'age' your creditors in exactly the same way as the debtors (see page 86). In this way it is possible to see at a

---

*In this example it is assumed that all materials have been purchased in the period in question.

glance which suppliers have been owed what sums of money, and for how long.

Stock control

Any manufacturing, subcontracting or assembling business will have to buy in raw materials and work on them to produce finished goods. They will have to keep track of three sorts of stock: raw materials, work in progress, and finished goods.

A retailing business will probably only be concerned with finished goods, and a service business may have no stocks at all.

If we assume that all High Note's stock is in finished goods, then the control ratio we can use is as follows:

$$\text{Days' finished goods stock} = \frac{\text{Finished goods stock}}{\text{Cost of sales*}} \times \text{Days in period}$$

For High Note in year 1 this would be:

$$\frac{10,000}{50,000} \times 365 = 73 \text{ days}$$

In year 2 the ratio would be 64 days.

It is impossible to make any general rules about stock levels. Obviously, a business has to carry enough stock to meet customers' demand, and a retail business must have it on display or on hand. However, if High Note's supplier can always deliver within 14 days it would be unnecessary to carry 73 days' stock.

The same basic equation can be applied to both raw materials and work-in-progress stock, but to reach raw materials stock you should substitute raw materials consumed for cost of sales. Once again the

---

*Cost of sales is used because it accurately reflects the amount of stock. The sales figure includes other items such as profit margin. If you are looking at an external company it is probable that the only figure available will be that for sales. In this case it can be used as an approximation.

strength of this ratio is that a business can quickly calculate how much it is costing to carry a given level of stock, in just the same way as customer credit costs were calculated earlier.

Cash control

The residual element in the control of working capital is cash or, if there is no cash left, the size of overdraft needed in a particular period.

Usually the amount of cash available to a small business is finite and specific, as also is the size of overdraft it can take, so stock levels, creditor and debtor policies, and other working capital elements are decided with these limits in mind. This information is assembled in the cash flow forecast, which was examined in greater detail in Chapter 3.

Circulation of working capital

The primary ratio for controlling working capital is usually considered to be the current ratio. This, however, is of more interest to outside bodies, such as bankers and suppliers wanting to see how safe their money is. The manager of a business is more interested in how well the money tied up in working capital is being used.

Look at High Note's balance sheets for the past two years. You can see that net current assets, another name for working capital, have shrunk from £16,410 to £14,000. Not too dramatic. Now let us look at these figures in relation to the level of business activity in each year.

$$\text{Circulation of working capital} = \frac{\text{Sales}}{\text{Working capital}}$$

$$\text{For year 1 this is } \frac{100,000}{16,410} = 6X, \text{ and year 2 } \frac{130,000}{14,000} = 9X$$

So we can see that not only has High Note got less money tied up in working capital in the second year, it has also used it more efficiently. In other words, it has circulated it faster. Each pound of working capital now produces £9 of sales, as opposed to only £6 last year. And as each pound of sales makes profit, the higher the sales, the higher the profit.

Averaging ratios

Ratios that involve the use of stock, debtors or creditors can be more accurately calculated by using the average of the opening and closing position. Seasonal factors or sales growth (contraction) will almost always make a single figure unrepresentative.

Look back to the High Note accounts on page 68. Here you can see an example where sales have grown by 30 per cent from £100,000 in the first year to £130,000 in the second. Obviously, neither the opening stock figure of £10,000 nor the closing stock of £12,000 is truly representative of what has happened in the intervening year. It seems much more likely that the average of the opening and closing stock figures is the best figure to use in calculating the stock control ratios shown on page 89. So in this example, £11,000 (10,000 + 12,000 ÷ 2) would be the figure to use.

Questions

1. What do you understand by the term 'overtrading'?
2. Using the Parkwood accounts on page 81, calculate the following ratios for both years:
   (a) the current ratio;
   (b) the quick ratio;
   (c) the average collection period (assuming all sales are on credit);
   (d) average days' stock held (assuming all stock is finished goods);
   (e) circulation of working capital.
3. Comment on the key changes in the ratios.

7 *Controlling fixed assets*

A major problem that all new or expanding businesses face is exactly how much to have of such items as equipment, storage capacity and work space. New *fixed assets* tend to be acquired in large chunks and are sometimes more opportunistic than market related in nature.

In any event, however, and for whatever reason acquired, once in the business it is important to make sure the asset is being effectively used. Controlling fixed assets splits down into two areas: looking at how effectively existing fixed assets are being used, and how to plan for new capital investments.

The fixed-asset pyramid

Generally, the best way to measure how well existing fixed assets are being used is to see how many pounds' worth of sales each pound of fixed assets is generating.

The overall ratio is that of Sales ÷ Fixed assets, which gives a measure of this use of the fixed assets.

Look back to the High Note accounts on pages 68–69. The use of fixed-asset ratio in that example is:

$$\text{Year 1} \quad \frac{100,000}{12,500} = 8X \qquad \text{Year 2} \quad \frac{130,000}{28,110} = 4.6X$$

This means that each pound invested in fixed assets has generated £8 worth of sales in year 1 and only £4.60 in year 2.

This 'inefficient' use of fixed assets has consumed all the benefit High Note gained from its improved use of working capital – and a little more. In fact, this is the main reason why the return on capital employed (ROCE) has declined in year 2. This may be a short-term problem which will be cured when expected new sales levels are reached: not at all unusual if, for example, a new piece of machinery was bought late in the second year.

Provided the rules outlined later in this chapter on planning capital investments are followed, this problem will correct itself. Otherwise a more detailed analysis may be needed.

Looking at the overall fixed-asset picture is rather like looking at the circulation of working capital ratio only as a means of monitoring working capital. Throughout Chapter 6 we looked at stock control, debtors and creditors as well. Fixed assets use is looked at both in total and in its component parts. A pyramid of ratios stretches out below this prime ratio.

The fixed-asset pyramid is shown in Figure 7.1, although the nature of the assets of a particular business may suggest others be included.

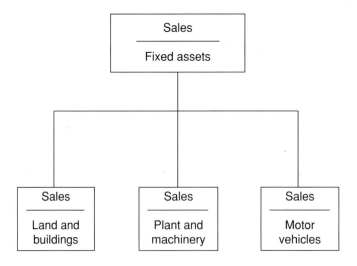

Figure 7.1 The fixed-asset pyramid

For example, a shop will also be interested in sales per square foot of selling space.

More detail still

More sophisticated businesses also monitor the output of individual pieces of equipment. They look at 'down time' (how long the equipment is out of commission), repair and maintenance costs, and the value of its output. If your business warrants it you can do this by simply expanding the pyramid as shown in Figure 7.2.

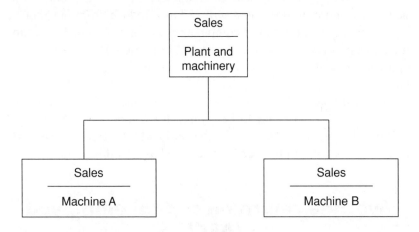

Figure 7.2   A detailed fixed-asset pyramid

Planning new capital investment

Most businesses discover quite early on that the equipment, machinery, space, etc that they started up with is not adequate for their future needs. That does not necessarily make the owners bad businesspeople; it just shows how difficult it is to predict the future shape of any business. Perhaps they prudently chose second-hand items, or they were extremely conservative in their sales forecasts, and now simply cannot meet the demand. In any event decisions have to be taken on new investments. Should existing equipment be replaced? Should more space be acquired?

If the answer to both these questions is yes, then decisions have to be made on which equipment or space should be chosen.

It is very rare that one piece of equipment is the only absolutely correct one for the job. Suppliers compete, and most products have significant differences. They may cost more but last longer, or cost less but be more expensive to run.

Work space in offices and shops also comes in different shapes, sizes and locations. All these capital decisions have two things in common. They usually involve (a) spending or committing a lump sum *now* to get (b) a stream of benefits in the future.

Anyone buying a new piece of equipment expects it to be used to help make more products that will in turn produce cash and profits. The same argument is true if equipment is being replaced. The equipment that produces the best return should be chosen. But how will it be chosen? What tools are available to help make a sound financial choice?

Clearly it is important to try and get these decisions right. After all, these types of assets tend to be around for a long time. Also, their resale value declines rapidly in the early years. Anyone who has bought a new car will not need further emphasis on this point.

Average return on capital employed (ARCE)

We know that one of the two primary objectives of a business is to make a satisfactory return on the capital employed in the business. Clearly, any new capital investment will have to achieve that same objective.

Until now we have only looked at the return on capital employed for an individual year. This would not be enough to see if a new investment proposal was worthwhile. Imagine your own reaction if someone asked you for £1,000 and explained only how they could return £200 at the end of the first year. You would expect them to come up with a complete proposal, one that covered the return of all the money you had lent – plus interest.

The same is true of any capital investment proposal. We have 'lent' the project, whatever it may be, a sum of capital. We expect a return on that capital over the working life of the assets bought. The ARCE method sets out to do just that. It measures the average profit over the life of a project and compares that with the capital employed.

Let us take an example to illustrate the method. A company is considered buying a new lathe for £5,000. The working life of the lathe will be five years, by which time it will be worthless. Net profit from the output of the lathe will come in as shown in Table 7.1.

Table 7.1   The ARCE method

Year		Net profit (after charging 100% depreciation) £
1		500
2		1,000
3		2,000
4		2,000
5		175
Total 5	years	5,675

Over the five years the capital invested in the lathe will produce an average return of £1,135 (5,675 ÷ 5) each year. As the capital concerned is £5,000 and the average return is £1,135, then the average return on the capital employed is 22.7 per cent or (1,135 ÷ 5,000) × 100.

This figure is simple to calculate and is of some help. For example, if on average the business buying the lathe is making a return of 30 per cent on capital employed, then buying the lathe will dilute the ROCE of the business as a whole.

Table 7.2 shows what happens to ROCE when the present business and the new project are 'merged' together to form the new business.

Table 7.2   Limitations of ARCE 1

Present business	+	New project	=	New business
	£	£		£
Average net profit	6,000	1,135		7,135
Capital employed	20,000	5,000		25,000
ROCE	30%	22.7%		28.5%

While this information is of some use as a tool for helping with capital investment decisions generally, ARCE has two severe limitations.

Let us suppose that the company has decided to buy a lathe – but there are two on offer. The first we have already examined. Profits from this lathe will build up gradually over the years and tail off sharply in the final year. The second lathe has rather different characteristics. It swings into action immediately, achieves high profits and tails off over the last three years (see Table 7.3).

Table 7.3   Limitations of ARCE 2

Year	Net profit from 2nd lathe (after charging 100 per cent depreciation)	1st lathe net profit
	£	£
1	2,650	500
2	2,650	1,000
4	125	2,000
3	125	2,000
5	125	175
Totals 5 years	5,675	5,675

As the overall total profits are the same, over the five years this investment will also produce an ARCE of 22.7 per cent. And yet, if all other factors were equal and only the figures on these pages had to be considered, most businesspeople would prefer the second lathe project. The reason they would give is that they get their profit in quicker. By the end of the second year that lathe would have paid for itself, while the first would not 'break even' until well into year 4.

This would be a 'gut reaction' and it would probably be right. That does not mean that gut reactions are better than financial techniques; it just means we have got the wrong technique. We need a technique that takes account of when the money comes in – clearly timing matters.

This leads into average rate of return's other major failing. It uses profit as one of the measures, although a business may have to wait months or even years for that profit to be realised as cash.

The other measure it uses is the cash spent on a capital investment, so like is not being compared with like: profit on the top of the equation and cash on the bottom. Two projects could generate identical profits, but if one generated those profits in immediate cash, the ARCE technique would not recognise it. But a businessperson's 'gut reaction' would once again choose the project that brought in the cash the soonest. And once again it'd be right.

Payback period

A more popular technique for evaluating capital investment decisions is the payback period method.

Payback attempts to overcome the fundamental weaknesses of the ARCE method. It compares the cash cost of the initial investment with the annual cash net inflows (or savings) that are generated by the investment. This goes beyond simply calculating profit as shown in the profit-and-loss account, which is governed by the realisation concept. The timing of the cash movements is calculated. That is, for example, when debtors will actually pay up, and when suppliers will have to be paid. By using cash in both elements it is comparing like with like.

Payback also attempts to deal with the timing issue by measuring the time taken for the initial cost to be recovered.

Table 7.4 illustrates the method.

Table 7.4   The payback method

	£
Initial cost of project	10,000
Annual net cash inflows	
Year 1	2,000
2	4,000
3	4,000
4	2,000
5	1,000

The payment period is three years. That is when the £10,000 initial cash cost has been matched by the annual net cash inflows of £2,000,

£4,000 and £4,000 of the first three years. Now we have a method that uses cash and takes some account of time.

Unfortunately it leaves us with a result that is difficult to compare directly with the profit performance of the rest of the business. If the business is currently making a 25 per cent return on capital employed, and a project has a payback period of three years, will the project enhance or reduce overall profitability? Without further calculation this question cannot be answered – and even then the answer will not necessarily be correct. Look again at the preceding example. The payback method looks only at the period taken to repay the initial investment. The following years are completely ignored, and yet the net cash inflows in those years are a benefit to the business, and their size matters.

This weakness is brought sharply into focus when competing projects are being compared.

Let us suppose your task is to choose between Projects A and B purely on financial criteria (see Table 7.5).

Table 7.5   Limitations of payback

	Project A £	Project B £
Initial cost of project	10,000	10,000
Annual net cash inflows		
Year 1	2,000	2,000
2	4,000	4,000
3	4,000	4,000
4	500	4,000
5	250	2,000
6	250	1,000
Total cash in flow	11,000	17,000
Payback period	3 years	3 years

The payback period for each proposal is three years, which signals that each project is equally acceptable on financial grounds. Clearly this is nonsense. It seems highly probable that Project B, which generates an extra £6,000 cash, is a better bet.

Payback has some merits, not least of which is its simplicity. It is often used as a cut-off criterion in the first stages of an evaluation. In other words, a business decides that it will not look at any project with a payback period greater than, say, four years. This provides a common starting point from which a more exacting comparison can be made. Beyond that use, the method's weaknesses make it a poor tool to use in investment decisions in a small business.

Big businesses do not expect to get all their capital investment decisions right. Small businesses have to, as their very survival depends on it.

Discounted cash flow

Neither the ARCE nor the payback method for evaluating capital investment projects is wholly satisfactory. They provide neither a sound technique for deciding whether or not to invest, nor a technique to help choose between competing projects. They fail for the reasons already described, but they also fail for a more fundamental reason.

The businessperson's gut feeling that timing is important is perhaps more true than he or she thinks. No one is going to invest a pound today, unless he or she expects to get back more than a pound at some future date. The level of that reward, if you like, is related in some way to the riskiness of the investment. But whatever the level of risk, no one wants less money back as that would involve making a loss.

The factor that alters the value of an investment over time is the interest rate. The longer the time period or the higher the interest rate, the larger is the final sum returned. This relationship between the initial sum invested and the sum finally returned is familarly known as compound interest.

The *compound interest equation* that calculates the precise figure for any interest rate or time period is:

Future value $= £P \times (1 + r)^{n}$

In this equation P = the initial sum invested, or principle, r = the interest rate expressed in decimals, and n = the time period in years.

So if we invest £100 for three years at 10 per cent we can expect a future value of:

$$£100 \times (1 + 0.1)^3$$
$$= £100 \times (1.1)^3$$
$$= £100 \times (1.1 \times 1.1 \times 1.1)$$
$$= £100 \times 1.331$$
$$= £133.10$$

For the doubters, the sum can be worked out in longhand (Table 7.6).

Table 7.6 Compound interest calculation

	Start £	Year 1 £	Year 2 £	Years 3 £
Balance brought forward	100.00	100.00	110.00	121.00
Interest at 10%		10.00	11.00	12.10
Value of investment	100.00	110.00	121.00	133.10
				~~Finish~~

You could consider the situation to be similar to looking through a telescope: looking forward in time through the compound interest equation magnifies the value of an investment.

But what happens when you look through the other end of a telescope? Images appear to shrink. To some extent this is similar to the problem a businessman might face when making up his mind about capital investment decisions. He knows he is not prepared to pay £1 now to get £1 back in the future; that would be bad business. What he has to calculate is exactly how much less than £1 he would pay to receive £1 back in, say, one year's time.

The thinking might go something like this. 'For this kind of investment I have to make 10 per cent profit, so I need to know what figure less 10 per cent will equal £1, and that is what I will pay now.' This is rather like moving to the other end of the telescope and looking backwards.

This problem is exactly the inverse of compounding and is called discounting. To calculate the appropriate discount factor we simply stand the compound interest equation on its head.

Discounting calculations

$$\frac{1}{(1+r)^n} = \frac{1}{(1+0.1)^1} = \frac{1}{1.1} = 0.909$$

So we would recommend that only £0.909 is paid today for £1 to be received in a year's time.

You can test the equation yourself by adding 10 per cent to £0.909. It should total £1.00.

Now we have an equation that lets us allow for the time value of money. (This is nothing whatever to do with the effects of inflation. Those effects are important and are covered later in this chapter.) Let us look at the ways to put the concept to use.

Present value

Just as the future value of an investment can be calculated using compounding, so the present value of cash coming in during the years ahead can be calculated using discounting.

We have already seen the heart of the present value equation. In full, using the same symbols as for compound interest, it is:

Present value equation

$$\text{Present value} = \pounds P \times \frac{1}{(1+r)^n}$$

The basic requirement of any present-value calculation is that you have some idea of what percentage profit you want from an investment. That is not usually a very difficult problem. If you have to borrow the money at 12 per cent, pay tax on the profits and take risks as well, it is not too hard to focus on an acceptable range of interest rates.

Alternatively, the yardsticks of current returns, competitors' or industry returns, or even a personal objective, can all be used to help arrive at an acceptable cut-off interest rate for discounting. Below this cut-off rate, a project is simply not acceptable.

Look at the following example. The proposition is that you should invest £50,000 now to make £80,000 over the next five years: a clear profit of £30,000, apparently a satisfactory situation. The cash will come in and out as shown in Table 7.7.

Table 7.7   Example showing the cash flow of investment

Year	Cash out £	Cash in £	Net cash flow £
0	50,000	–	(50,000)
1	5,000	15,000	10,000
2	5,000	15,000	10,000
3	12,500	37,500	25,000
4	12,500	37,500	25,000
5	5,000	15,000	10,000
			30,000

This is based on a £50,000 investment now, followed by some cash expenses and cash income in the future. In other words, a typical business buying in materials, adding value and selling mainly on monthly terms. The fourth column shows the net cash flow for each year of the project's life. Cash in exceeds cash out by £30,000 – in other words the profit.

However, we know that the net cash flow received in future years is not worth as much as present pounds. Remember, no businessperson will pay £1 now to receive only £1 back in the future. Our problem is to discount all the future cash flows back to present values, in exactly the same manner as we did on page 102.

Once again we could use our present value equation, but that would be rather time consuming. Fortunately there are tables that do all the sums for us, and this facility is becoming increasingly available on calculators. A set of these tables is shown on pages 120–23.

All we have to decide on how is a discount rate. Well, if we know we can have a risk-free investment of 12 per cent, it may not seem worthwhile taking a risk unless we can make 17 per cent, a modest enough figure for a risk project.

Using the discount tables we can select the appropriate year and interest rate, to arrive at the present value factor (Table 7.8).

Table 7.8 Example showing the present value of cash flow of investment

Year	Net cash flow £	Present value factor at 17%	Net present value £
0	(50,000)	1.000	(50,000)
1	10,000	0.855	8,550
2	10,000	0.731	7,310
3	25,000	0.624	15,600
4	25,000	0.534	13,350
5	10,000	0.456	4,560
			(630)

Take the present value factor for each year and multiply it by the net cash flow. This gives the net present value of the cash that this investment generates. In this case it comes to £49,370 (8,550 + 7,310 + 15,600 + 13,350 + 4,560), which is £630 less than the £50,000 we put in. So if you had expected to make 17 per cent return on your investment, you would have been disappointed.

Interestingly enough both the ARCE and payback methods would probably have encouraged you to go ahead. ARCE would have come up with average profits of £16,000 per annum, which represents a 32 per cent return on capital employed, and the payback period is 3 years and 2½ months – not long at all. But the fatal flaw in both these methods is revealed clearly by the present value concept. The timing of the cash flow over the working life of the investment is crucial, and that must form the central part of any judgement on whether or not to invest.

The profitability index

Present value is clearly a superior capital investment appraisal method, overcoming the weaknesses of the other two techniques. But in its present form it only provides the answer to our first question. Should we invest or not? Having decided on the level of return (interest) we want, and calculated the net cash flow, we simply discount to arrive at the net present value. If this is greater than zero, then the project is acceptable.

Suppose, like our problem with the lathes, the question is not simply whether or not to invest, but also to choose between alternatives, then would the present value method work? This fairly extreme example (Table 7.9) will highlight the difficulty of using the present value method alone to solve both types of problem.

Table 7.9 Comparing projects using the present value method

	Project A			Project B		
Year	Net cash flow	Present value factor at 10%	Net present value	Net cash flow	Present value factor at 10%	Net present value
	£		£	£		£
0	(7,646)	1.000	(7,646)	(95,720)	1.000	(95,720)
1	3,000	0.909	2,727	30,000	0.909	27,270
2	4,000	0.826	3,304	40,000	0.826	33,040
3	5,000	0.751	3,755	50,000	0.751	37,550
	Present value		9,786	Present value		97,860
	Net present value		2,140	Net present value		2,140

Here we have two possible projects to investment in. One calls for capital of £7,646 and the other for £95,720. Leaving aside the problem of finding the money, which is the better investment proposition? If we are happy with making a 10 per cent return on our investment, then both projects are acceptable. Both end up with a net present value of £2,140, so that cannot be the deciding factor. Yet it is clear that A is a better bet than B, simply because the relationship between the size of the investment and the present value of the cash flow is 'better'.

The way these elements are related is through the profitability index, which is set out below:

The profitability index

$$\text{Profitability index} = \frac{\text{Present value of earnings}}{\text{Cost of investment}}$$

In this example the index for Project A is 128 per cent (9,786 ÷ 7,646), and for B 102 per cent (97,860 ÷ 95,720). The profitability index clearly signals that Project A is the better choice.

In fact, any comparison of projects that do not have identical initial investments and lifetimes can only be properly made using the profitability index.

To summarise then, the first step is to see if the various possible projects are acceptable by discounting their net cash flows at the cut-off interest rate. If a choice has to be made between the acceptable projects, calculate each one's profitability index, and then rank them as shown on Table 7.10.

Table 7.10   Example showing project ranking by profitability index

Project	Profitability index %
A	135
B	127
C	117
D	104
E	101

It is not possible to have a profitability index lower than 100 per cent. That would imply a negative net present value, which in turn would eliminate the proposal at the first stage of the evaluation process.

Internal rate of return

One important piece of information has not been provided by either the net present value or the profitability index. A capital investment proposal may have a satisfactory net present value, that is a positive one, at our cut-off interest rate. It may also come out ahead of other choices in the profitability index ranking, but we still do not know exactly what rate of return we can expect to get.

This is important information for three main reasons. First, it allows us to compare new investment proposals with the rest of the business, something that neither present value nor the profitability index will do. Second, it gives us a yardstick understood by people outside the business. For example, bankers or other potential investors will understand a proposal for funds with a straightforward percentage as the end result. They will not be so sure of a figure such as £1,000 net present value. This could be misunderstood for the total profit, and be rejected. Finally, under most circumstances, the internal rate of return, as this is known, is a satisfactory method of comparing projects. (In any doubtful situations the profitability index will be the deciding factor.)

We do know, however, that the rate of return must be greater than the cut-off interest rate, provided, of course, that the net present value is positive.

Table 7.11 shows how Project A's net present value was calculated in the profitability index example.

Table 7.11 Calculating the internal rate of return 1

Year	Net cash flow £	Present value factor at 10%	Net present value £
0	(7,646)	1.000	(7,646)
1	3,000	0.909	2,727
2	4,000	0.826	3,304
3	5,000	0.751	3,755
		Present value	9,786
		Net present value	2,140

We know that Project A is expected to make a rate of return higher than 10 per cent simply because the net present value is positive. If we increase the present value to, say, 20 per cent by arbitrarily raising our cut-off level, we can see whether it meets that test (Table 7.12).

Table 7.12   Calculating the internal rate of return 2

Year	Net cash flow £	Present value factor at 20%	Net present value £
0	(7,646)	1.000	(7,646)
1	3,000	0.833	2,499
2	4,000	0.694	2,776
3	5,000	0.579	2,895
		Present value	8,170
		Net present value	524

We can see that the project still shows a positive net present value at our new cut-off rate of 20 per cent. However, the figure is much smaller and suggests we are getting close to the 'internal rate of return'. That is the discount rate which, when applied to the net cash flow, results in a zero net present value. We could go on experimenting to reach that rate, but this would be time consuming, and not very rewarding, for reasons explained at the end of the chapter.

There is a simple technique known as interpolating, which we can use providing we have one positive and one negative net present value figure.

This is how interpolation works: let us select a discount rate that we are reasonably certain will lead to a negative net present value, for example 25 per cent (Table 7.13).

Table 7.13   Calculating the internal rate of return 3

Year	Net cash flow £	Present value factor at 25%	Net present value £
0	(7,646)	1.000	(7,646)
1	3,000	0.800	2,400
2	4,000	0.640	2,560
3	5,000	0.512	2,560
		Present value	7,520
		Net present value	(126)

Now we know that the internal rate of return must lie between 20 and 25 per cent. That is because the project had a positive net present value at 20 per cent and a negative one at 25 per cent. Using the interpolation equation we can arrive at a good approximation of the discount rate.

Interpolation equation

$$\begin{matrix} \text{Internal} \\ \text{rate of} \\ \text{return (IRR)} \\ \text{Rate of trial} \end{matrix} = \begin{matrix} \text{Lowest} \\ \text{trial} \\ \text{rate} \end{matrix} + \left[\frac{\text{Positive cash flow}}{\text{Range of cash flow}} \times \begin{matrix} \text{Difference between} \\ \text{high and low rates} \end{matrix} \right] \%$$

For this example the equation would be:

$$\text{IRR} = 20 + \left[\frac{524}{524 + 126} \times (25 - 20) \right] \%$$

$$= 20 + 4.03\% = 24.03\%* = 24\%$$

---

*It is normal practice to use only whole numbers when calculating rates of return.

Had we used the net present value figure from the 10 per cent discount calculation, we would have arrived at a different IRR. The reason is that to give an accurate IRR figure, both net present value figures used in the interpolation equation must be fairly small.

You will have an opportunity to prove both that the equation works and that it is more accurate with low figures, at the end of the chapter.

Risk and sensitivity analysis

Discounted cash flow (DCF) gives us a sound tool for deciding whether an investment proposal is acceptable or not. It also helps us to choose between competing projects. DCF can perform one more important task: it can be used to examine the circumstances that could make a project *unacceptable*.

Look back at Table 7.12. If the cut-off interest rate is 20 per cent, this project is acceptable. The net cash flow has been calculated on a series of assumptions about sales levels, days' credit taken and given, expenses, etc. But what if any one of those assumptions is wrong? For example, supposing debtors pay up much more slowly and the resultant cash flow takes longer to build up – but of course lasts longer, with some people not paying up until year 4?

Table 7.14 shows how the cash flow will look if these new 'assumptions' occur.

Table 7.14   Example of a sensitivity analysis

Year	First estimate of net cash flow £	New estimate of net cash flow £	Present value factor at 20%	Net present value £
0	(7,646)	(7,646)	1.000	(7,646)
1	3,000	2,000	0.833	1,666
2	4,000	3,000	0.694	2,082
3	5,000	4,000	0.579	2,316
4		3,000	0.482	1,446
Total positive cash flow	12,000	12,000	Present value	7,510
			Net present value	(136)

Under these circumstances the investment would not be acceptable, so now we know how 'sensitive' the project is to customers paying up promptly. We have to assess what the risk is of these new circumstances occurring.

The same technique can be applied to any of the assumptions built into the cash-flow forecast, and a good, or robust, investment proposal is one that can withstand a range of 'what if…?'-type tests.

Dealing with inflation

A common assumption is that varying the discounted cash-flow cut-off point is a good way to deal with inflation. For example, if you felt that 20 per cent was a good rate of return last year, and inflation is set to be 6 per cent next year, then 26 per cent should be the new cut-off rate.

Although attractively simple, the logic is wrong. Inflation is already dealt with in the assumptions built into the cash-flow forecast (or it certainly should be). For example, the sum covering payments for materials is based on three assumptions: the volume of materials needed, how much they will cost, and when they will be paid for. The middle assumption here is where inflation is allowed for.

Discounted cash flow in working capital decisions

So far we have treated DCF as though it were exclusively for looking at investments in fixed assets. Any investment in fixed assets almost inevitably has an effect on working capital levels. DCF techniques have to be able to accommodate both fixed and working capital factors in investment decisions. Working through the following case study will show how DCF is used under these circumstances.

Launching a new product: a capital budgeting case study

Your marketing director is actively considering the launch of a new product. The following information on likely revenues and expenses has been obtained to help in the decision.

Production costs

The new product will require new equipment costing £250,000 and alterations to existing buildings and plant layout costing £120,000.

Sales forecasts and gross margins

The long-range plan (LRP) for the new product (Table 7.15) expects sales to grow to £1.2m by the fifth year, with gross marketing margin running at 60 per cent.

Table 7.15   Long-range plan for a new product

Year	Sales forecast (cash) £	Cash generated by new product £
1	200,000	120,000
2	400,000	240,000
3	800,000	480,000
4	1,000,000	600,000
5	1,200,000	720,000

The sales of this product are not expected to eat into sales of existing products.

Marketing and sales expenses

You expect advertising and promotional expenditure to be heaviest in the first two years, tailing off to a relatively low figure later (see Table 7.16).

Table 7.16   Promotional expenditure for a new product

Year	£
1	150,000
2	200,000
3	100,000
4	70,000
5	50,000

t new sales people will be recruited to promote the
e start of year 2 and the remainder at the start of year
son costs the company £18,700 per annum (that

Debtors and stocks

These are expected to build up over the five years to a total of
£220,000, about 20 per cent of sales. At the end of each year, the
amounts of extra cash shown in Table 7.17 will be required to finance
debtors and stocks.

Table 7.17   Cash needed to finance debtors and stocks of a new
product

Year	£
1	40,000
2	40,000
3	80,000
4	40,000
5	20,000
Total investment by year 5 =	220,000

Company profit required

The company is unlikely to sanction a proposal generating less than 25
per cent on a DCF basis.

Case study assignment questions

1. Work out the net cash flow for each year from year 0 to year 5
   inclusive.
2. Calculate the net present value (NPV) at the present 25 per cent
   discount rate.
3. What is the internal rate of return (IRR) of the project?

Use the worksheet provided. If you get stuck, look at the solution,
which will show the logic and answer.

Launching a new product – worksheet

1. Annual cash flows   2. Cash flow discounted at 25%

Year		Cash out £	Cash in £	Net cash flow £	Discount rate 25% £	Discounted cash flow £	Discount at 20% £	Discounted cash flow £
0	Production				1.000		1.000	
1	Promotion							
	Debtors and stock				0.800		0.833	
2	Promotion							
	Salespeople							
	Debtors and stock				0.640		0.694	
3	Promotion							
	Salespeople							
	Debtors and stock				0.512		0.579	
4	Promotion							
	Salespeople							
	Debtors and stock				0.410		0.482	
5	Promotion							
	Salespeople							
	Debtors and stock				0.328		0.402	

3. The internal rate of return

True rate = [   ] % =

Launching a new product – solution

1. Annual cash flows

2. Cash flow discounted at 25%

Year		Cash out £	Cash in £	Net cash flow £	Discount rate 25% £	Discounted cash flow £	Discount at 20% £	Discounted cash flow £
0	Production	370,000	0	(370,000)	1.000	(370,000)	1.000	(370,000)
		370,000						
1	Promotion	150,000						
	Debtors and stock	40,000						
		190,000	120,000	(70,000)	0.800	(56,000)	0.833	(58,310)
2	Promotion	200,000						
	Salespeople	74,800						
	Debtors and stock	40,000						
		314,800	240,000	(74,800)	0.640	(47,872)	0.694	(51,911)
3	Promotion	100,000						
	Salespeople	74,800						
	Debtors and stock	80,000						
		254,800	480,000	225,200	0.512	115,302	0.579	130,391
4	Promotion	70,000						
	Salespeople	149,600						
	Debtors and stock	40,000						
		259,600	600,000	340,400	0.410	139,564	0.482	164,073
5	Promotion	50,000						
	Salespeople	149,600						
	Debtors and stock	20,000						
		219,600	720,000	500,400	0.328	164,131	0.402	201,161
						(54,875)		15,403

3. The internal rate of return

$$\text{True rate} = 20 + \left[\frac{15,403}{70,278} \right] \times 5\% = 21.10\%$$

So don't invest if you want to make 25 per cent.

Some general factors in investment decisions

Some considerable space has been devoted to the subject of new investment appraisal. It is an area where many small businesses get into fatal problems very early on. People starting up rarely have a proper framework for deciding how much money to invest in a business idea. They are usually more concerned with how to raise the money. A critical look using discounted cash flow would probably change their minds, both about how much to spend on starting up and on expansion.

However, in the end, any investment appraisal is only as good as the information that is used to build up the cash-flow forecast. Much of the benefit in using DCF is that it forces investors to think through the whole decision thoroughly.

The bulk of the work in investment appraisal is concerned with:

1. Assessing market size, market share, market growth and selling price.
2. Estimating and phasing the initial cost of the investment; working life of facilities; working capital requirements.
3. Assessing of plant output rate.
4. Ensuring that the provision of additional services and ancillaries has not been overlooked.
5. Estimating operating costs.
6. Estimating the rate of taxation.
7. Estimating the residual value of the asset.

The relatively simple task is that of using sound investment appraisal techniques.

A general purpose DCF worksheet is provided on page 119 for use with your own projects, and the following questions.

Questions

1. Test the interpolated IRR rate of 24 per cent on page 110 to prove it is correct.
2. Use 10 per cent as the lowest trial rate in the interpolation

equation on page 110 to show that the nearer the net present values are to zero, the more accurate the interpolation.

3. You have to choose between the following two machines. Each has an expected life of five years and will result in net cash flows (savings) as follows:

	Machine A £	Machine B £
Cost	12,500	15,000
Net cash flow		
Year 1	2,000	3,000
2	4,000	6,000
3	5,000	5,000
4	2,500	3,000
5	2,000	2,000
Residual value	1,500	2,500

To help you make your choice, calculate:

(a) The net present value of each machine at the 10 and 15 per cent discount rates.
(b) Their respective internal rates of return.
(c) Their profitability indices at the 10 per cent discount factor.

What is your choice?

General purpose DCF working sheet

Time in years from today	Cash outflow £	Cash inflow £	Net cash flow £	Discount factor	% Present value	Discount factor	% Present value	Discount factor	% Present value	Cash flow discounted at: Discount factor	% Present value	Discount factor	% Present value
0													
1													
2													
3													
4													
5													
6													
7													
8													
9													
10													
11													
12													
13													
14													
15													

Net present value

Interpolating to deduce true rate of return

$$\text{True rate} = \text{Lowest trial rate} + \left[\frac{\text{Positive cash flow}}{\text{Range of cash flow}} \times \text{Difference between high and low rates} \right] \%$$

Discount tables

The present value of 1

Year					Percentage					
	1	2	3	4	5	6	7	8	9	10
1	0.990099	0.980392	0.970874	0.961538	0.952381	0.943396	0.934579	0.925926	0.917431	0.909091
2	0.980296	0.961169	0.942596	0.925556	0.907029	0.889996	0.873439	0.857339	0.841680	0.826446
3	0.970590	0.942322	0.915142	0.888996	0.863838	0.839619	0.816298	0.793832	0.772183	0.751315
4	0.960980	0.923845	0.888487	0.854804	0.822702	0.792094	0.762895	0.735030	0.708425	0.683013
5	0.951466	0.905731	0.862609	0.821927	0.783526	0.747258	0.712986	0.680583	0.649931	0.620921
6	0.942045	0.887971	0.837484	0.790315	0.746215	0.704961	0.666342	0.630170	0.596267	0.564474
7	0.932718	0.870560	0.813092	0.759918	0.710681	0.665057	0.622750	0.583490	0.547034	0.513158
8	0.923483	0.853490	0.789409	0.730690	0.676839	0.627412	0.582009	0.540269	0.501866	0.466507
9	0.914340	0.836755	0.766417	0.702587	0.644609	0.591898	0.543934	0.500249	0.460428	0.424098
10	0.905287	0.820348	0.744094	0.675564	0.613913	0.558395	0.508349	0.463193	0.422411	0.385543
11	0.896324	0.804263	0.722421	0.649581	0.584679	0.526788	0.475093	0.428883	0.387533	0.350494
12	0.887449	0.788493	0.701380	0.624597	0.556837	0.496969	0.444012	0.397114	0.355535	0.318631
13	0.878663	0.773033	0.680951	0.600574	0.530321	0.468839	0.414964	0.367698	0.326179	0.289664
14	0.869963	0.757875	0.661118	0.577475	0.505068	0.442301	0.387817	0.340461	0.299246	0.263331
15	0.861349	0.743015	0.641862	0.555265	0.481017	0.417265	0.362446	0.315242	0.274538	0.239392
16	0.852821	0.728446	0.623167	0.533908	0.458112	0.393646	0.338735	0.291890	0.251870	0.217629
17	0.844377	0.174163	0.605016	0.513373	0.436297	0.371364	0.316574	0.270269	0.231073	0.197845
18	0.836017	0.700159	0.587395	0.493628	0.415521	0.350344	0.295864	0.250249	0.211994	0.179859
19	0.827740	0.686431	0.570286	0.474642	0.395734	0.330513	0.276508	0.231712	0.194490	0.163508
20	0.819544	0.672971	0.553676	0.456387	0.376889	0.311805	0.258419	0.214548	0.178431	0.148644

					Percentage					
Year	11	12	13	14	15	16	17	18	19	20
1	0.900901	0.892857	0.884956	0.877193	0.869565	0.862069	0.854701	0.847458	0.840336	0.833333
2	0.811622	0.797194	0.783147	0.769468	0.756144	0.743163	0.730514	0.718184	0.706165	0.694444
3	0.731191	0.711780	0.693050	0.674972	0.657516	0.640658	0.624371	0.608631	0.593416	0.578704
4	0.658731	0.635518	0.613319	0.592080	0.571753	0.552291	0.533650	0.515789	0.498669	0.482253
5	0.593451	0.567427	0.542760	0.519369	0.497177	0.476113	0.456111	0.437109	0.419049	0.401878
6	0.534641	0.506631	0.480319	0.455587	0.432328	0.410442	0.389839	0.370432	0.352142	0.334898
7	0.481658	0.452349	0.425061	0.399637	0.375937	0.353830	0.333195	0.313925	0.295918	0.279082
8	0.433926	0.403883	0.376160	0.350559	0.326902	0.305025	0.284782	0.266038	0.248671	0.232568
9	0.390925	0.360610	0.332885	0.307508	0.284262	0.262953	0.243404	0.225456	0.208967	0.193807
10	0.352184	0.321973	0.294588	0.269744	0.247185	0.226684	0.208037	0.191064	0.175602	0.161506
11	0.317283	0.287476	0.260698	0.236617	0.214943	0.195417	0.177810	0.161919	0.147565	0.134588
12	0.285841	0.256675	0.230706	0.207559	0.186907	0.168463	0.151974	0.137220	0.124004	0.112157
13	0.257514	0.229174	0.204165	0.182069	0.162528	0.145227	0.129892	0.116288	0.104205	0.093464
14	0.231995	0.204620	0.180677	0.159710	0.141329	0.125195	0.111019	0.098549	0.087567	0.077887
15	0.209004	0.182696	0.159891	0.140096	0.122894	0.107927	0.094888	0.083516	0.073586	0.064905
16	0.188292	0.163122	0.141496	0.122892	0.106865	0.093041	0.081101	0.070776	0.061837	0.054088
17	0.169663	0.145644	0.125218	0.107800	0.092926	0.080207	0.069317	0.059980	0.051964	0.045073
18	0.152822	0.130040	0.110812	0.094561	0.080805	0.069144	0.059245	0.050830	0.043667	0.037561
19	0.137678	0.116107	0.098064	0.082948	0.070265	0.059607	0.050637	0.043077	0.036695	0.031301
20	0.124043	0.103667	0.086782	0.072762	0.061100	0.051385	0.043280	0.036506	0.030836	0.026084

				Percentage					
Year	21	22	23	24	25	26	27	28	29	30
1	0.826446	0.819672	0.813008	0.806452	0.800000	0.793651	0.787402	0.781250	0.775194	0.769231
2	0.683013	0.671862	0.660982	0.650364	0.640000	0.629882	0.620001	0.610352	0.600925	0.591716
3	0.564474	0.550707	0.537384	0.524487	0.512000	0.499906	0.488190	0.476837	0.465834	0.455166
4	0.466507	0.451399	0.436897	0.422974	0.409600	0.396751	0.384402	0.372529	0.361111	0.350128
5	0.385543	0.369999	0.355201	0.341108	0.327680	0.314882	0.302678	0.291038	0.279931	0.269329
6	0.318631	0.303278	0.288781	0.275087	0.262144	0.249906	0.238329	0.227374	0.217001	0.207176
7	0.263331	0.248589	0.234782	0.221844	0.209715	0.198338	0.187661	0.177636	0.168218	0.159366
8	0.217629	0.203761	0.190879	0.178907	0.167772	0.157411	0.147765	0.138778	0.130401	0.122589
9	0.179859	0.167017	0.155187	0.144280	0.134218	0.124930	0.116350	0.108420	0.101086	0.094300
10	0.148644	0.136899	0.126168	0.116354	0.107374	0.099150	0.091614	0.084703	0.078362	0.072538
11	0.122846	0.112213	0.102576	0.093834	0.085899	0.078691	0.072137	0.066174	0.060745	0.055799
12	0.101526	0.091978	0.083395	0.075673	0.068719	0.062453	0.056801	0.051699	0.047089	0.042922
13	0.083905	0.075391	0.067801	0.061026	0.054976	0.049566	0.044725	0.040390	0.036503	0.033017
14	0.069343	0.061796	0.055122	0.049215	0.043980	0.039338	0.035217	0.031554	0.028297	0.025398
15	0.057309	0.050653	0.044815	0.039689	0.035184	0.031221	0.027730	0.024652	0.021936	0.019537
16	0.047362	0.041519	0.036435	0.032008	0.028147	0.024778	0.021834	0.019259	0.017005	0.015028
17	0.039143	0.034032	0.029622	0.025813	0.022518	0.019665	0.017192	0.015046	0.013182	0.011560
18	0.032349	0.027895	0.024083	0.020817	0.018014	0.015607	0.013537	0.011755	0.010218	0.008892
19	0.026735	0.022865	0.019580	0.016788	0.014412	0.012387	0.010659	0.009184	0.007921	0.006840
20	0.022095	0.018741	0.015918	0.013538	0.011529	0.009831	0.008393	0.007175	0.006141	0.005262

| | | | | | *Percentage* | | | | | |
Year	*31*	*32*	*33*	*34*	*35*	*36*	*37*	*38*	*39*	*40*
1	0.763359	0.757576	0.751880	0.746269	0.740741	0.735294	0.729927	0.724638	0.719424	0.714286
2	0.582717	0.573921	0.565323	0.556917	0.548697	0.540657	0.532793	0.525100	0.517572	0.510204
3	0.444822	0.434789	0.425055	0.415610	0.406442	0.397542	0.388900	0.380507	0.372354	0.354431
4	0.339559	0.329385	0.319590	0.310156	0.301068	0.292310	0.283869	0.275730	0.267880	0.260309
5	0.259205	0.249534	0.240293	0.231460	0.223014	0.214934	0.207204	0.199804	0.192720	0.185934
6	0.197866	0.189041	0.180672	0.172731	0.165195	0.158040	0.151243	0.144786	0.138647	0.132810
7	0.151043	0.143213	0.135843	0.128904	0.122367	0.116206	0.110397	0.104917	0.099746	0.094865
8	0.115300	0.108495	0.102138	0.096197	0.090642	0.085445	0.080582	0.076027	0.071760	0.067760
9	0.088015	0.082193	0.076795	0.071789	0.067142	0.062828	0.058819	0.055092	0.051626	0.048400
10	0.067187	0.062267	0.057741	0.053574	0.049735	0.046197	0.042933	0.039922	0.037141	0.034572
11	0.051288	0.047172	0.043414	0.039980	0.036841	0.033968	0.031338	0.028929	0.026720	0.024694
12	0.039151	0.035737	0.032642	0.029836	0.027289	0.024977	0.022875	0.020963	0.019223	0.017639
13	0.029886	0.027073	0.024543	0.022266	0.020214	0.018365	0.016697	0.015190	0.013830	0.012599
14	0.022814	0.020510	0.018453	0.016616	0.014974	0.013504	0.012187	0.011008	0.009949	0.008999
15	0.017415	0.015538	0.013875	0.012400	0.011092	0.009929	0.008896	0.007977	0.007158	0.006428
16	0.013294	0.011771	0.010432	0.009254	0.008216	0.007301	0.006493	0.005780	0.005149	0.004591
17	0.010148	0.008918	0.007844	0.006906	0.006086	0.005368	0.004740	0.004188	0.003705	0.003280
18	0.007747	0.006756	0.005898	0.005154	0.004508	0.003947	0.003460	0.003035	0.002665	0.002343
19	0.005914	0.005118	0.004434	0.003846	0.003339	0.002902	0.002525	0.002199	0.001917	0.001673
20	0.004514	0.003877	0.003334	0.002870	0.002474	0.002134	0.001843	0.001594	0.001379	0.001195

8 *Costs, volume, pricing and profit decisions*

In the preceding chapters we have seen how business controls can be developed. These can be used to monitor performance against the fundamental objectives of profitability, and the business's capacity to survive. So far we have taken certain decisions for granted and ignored how to cost the product or service we are marketing, and indeed, how to set the selling price. These decisions are clearly very important if you want to be sure of making a profit.

Adding up the costs

At first glance the problem is simple. You just add up all the costs and charge a bit more. The more you charge above your costs, provided the customers will keep on buying, the more profit you make.

Unfortunately as soon as you start to do the sums the problem gets a little more complex. For a start, not all costs have the same characteristics. Some costs, for example, do not change however much you sell. If you are running a shop, the rent and rates are relatively constant figures, completely independent of the volume of your sales. On the other hand, the cost of the products sold from the shop is completely dependent on volume. The more you sell, the more it costs you to buy in stock.

You can't really add up those two types of costs until you have made an assumption about volume – how much you plan to sell.

	£
Rent and rates for shop	2,500
Cost of 1,000 units of volume of product	1,000
Total costs	3,500

Look at the simple example above. Until we decide to buy, and we hope sell, 1,000 units of our product, we cannot total the costs.

With the volume hypothesised we can arrive at a cost per unit of product of:

Total costs ÷ Number of units
= £3,500   ÷ 1,000   = £3.50

Now, provided we sell out all the above at £3.50, we shall always be profitable. But will we? Suppose we do not sell all the 1,000 units, what then? With a selling price of £4.50 we could, in theory, make a profit of £1,000 if we sell all 1,000 units. That is a total sales revenue of £4,500, minus total costs of £3,500. But if we only sell 500 units, out total revenue drops to £2,250 and we actually lose £1,250* (total revenue £2,250 – total costs £3,500). So at one level of sales a selling price of £4.50 is satisfactory, and at another it is a disaster.

This very simple example shows that all those decisions are intertwined. Costs, sales volume, selling prices and profits are all linked together. A decision taken in any one of these areas has an impact on the other areas.

To understand the relationship between these factors, we need a picture or model of how they link up. Before we can build up this model, we need some more information on each of the component parts of cost.

The components of cost

Understanding the behaviour of costs as the trading patterns in a business change is an area of vital importance to decision makers. It is this 'dynamic' nature in every business that makes good costing decisions the key to survival. The last example showed that if the situation was

---

* The loss may not be as dramatic as that because we may still have the product available to sell later, but if it is fresh vegetables, for example, we will not. In any event, stored products attract new costs, such as warehousing and finance charges.

static and predictable, a profit was certain, but if any one component in the equation was not a certainty (in that example it was volume), then the situation was quite different.

To see how costs behave under changing conditions we first have to identify the different type of cost.

Fixed costs

Fixed costs are costs that happen, by and large, whatever the level of activity. For example, the cost of buying a car is the same whether it is driven 100 miles a year or 20,000 miles. The same is also true of the road tax, the insurance and any extras, such as a radio.

In a business, as well as the cost of buying cars, there are other fixed costs such as plant, equipment, computers, desks, and answering machines. But certain less tangible items can also be fixed costs, for example, rent, rates, insurance, etc, which are usually set quite independent of how successful or otherwise a business is.

Costs such as most of those mentioned above are fixed irrespective of the timescale under consideration. Other costs, such as those of employing people, while theoretically variable in the short term, in practice are fixed. In other words, if sales demand goes down and a business needs fewer people, the costs cannot be shed for several weeks (notice, holiday pay, redundancy, etc). Also, if the people involved are highly skilled or expensive to recruit and train (or in some other way particularly valuable) and the downturn looks a short one, it may not be cost effective to reduce those short-run costs in line with falling demand. So viewed over a period of weeks and months, labour is a fixed cost. Over a longer period it may not be fixed.

We could draw a simple chart showing how fixed costs behave as the 'dynamic' volume changes. The first phase of our cost model is shown overleaf (Figure 8.1).

This shows a static level of fixed costs over a particular range of output. To return to a previous example, this could show the fixed cost, rent and rates for a shop to be constant over a wide range of sales levels.

Once the shop owner has reached a satisfactory sales and profit level in one shop, he or she may decide to rent another one, in which case the fixed costs will 'step' up. This can be shown in the variation on the fixed cost model overleaf (Figure 8.2).

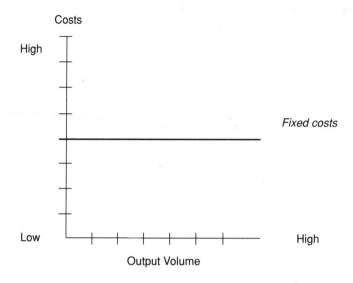

Figure 8.1 Cost model 1: showing fixed costs

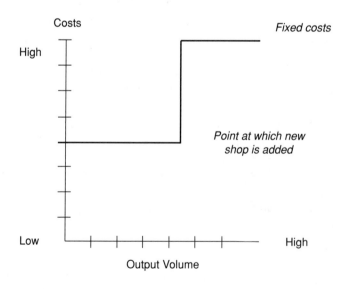

Figure 8.2 Variation on cost model 1: showing a 'step up' in fixed costs

Variable costs

These are costs that change in line with output. Raw materials for production, packaging materials, bonuses, piece rates, sales commission and postage are some examples. The important characteristic of a variable cost is that it rises or falls in direct proportion to any growth or decline in output volumes.

We can now draw a chart showing how variable costs behave as volume changes. The second phase of our cost model will look like Figure 8.3.

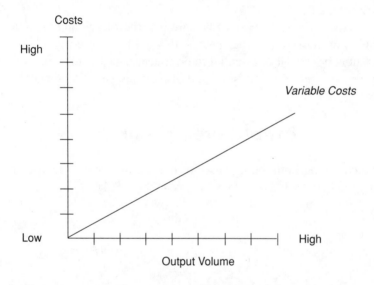

Figure 8.3   Cost model 2: showing behaviour of variable costs as volume changes

There is a popular misconception that defines fixed costs as those costs that are predictable, and variable costs as those that are subject to change at any moment. The definitions already given are the only valid ones for costing purposes.

Semi-variable costs

Unfortunately not all costs fit easily into either the fixed or variable category.

Some costs have both a fixed and a variable element. For example, a telephone has a quarterly rental cost which is fixed, and a cost per unit consumed which is variable. In this particular example low consumers can be seriously penalised. If only a few calls are made each month, their total cost per call (fixed rental + cost per unit ÷ number of calls) can be several pounds.

Other examples of this dual-component cost are photocopier rentals, electricity and gas.

These semi-variable costs must be split into their fixed and variable elements. For most small businesses this will be a fairly simple process; nevertheless it is essential to do it accurately or else much of the purpose and benefits of this method of cost analysis will be wasted.

Break-even point

Now we can bring both these phases of the costing model together to show the total costs, and how they behave (Figure 8.4).

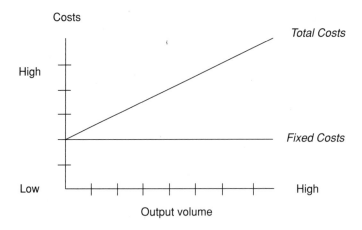

Figure 8.4 Cost model showing total costs and fixed costs

By starting the variable costs from the plateau of the fixed costs, we can produce a line showing the total costs. Taking vertical and horizontal lines from any point in the total cost line will give the total costs for any chosen output volume. This is an essential feature of the costing model that lets us see how costs change with different output volumes: in other words, accommodating the dynamic nature of a business.

It is to be hoped that we are not simply producing things and creating costs. We are also selling things and creating income. So a further line can be added to the model to show sales revenue as it comes in. To help bring the model to life, let's add some figures, for illustration purposes only.

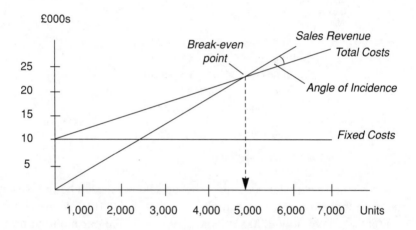

Figure 8.5   Cost model showing a break-even point

Figure 8.5 shows the break-even point (BEP). Perhaps the most important single calculation in the whole costing exercise is to find the point at which real profits start to be made.

The point where the sales revenue line crosses the total costs line is the break-even point. It is only after that point has been reached that a business can start to make a profit. We can work this out by drawing a graph, such as the example above, or by using a simple formula. The advantage of using the formula as well is that you can experiment by changing the values of some of the elements in the model quickly.

The equation for the BEP is:

$$BEP = \frac{\text{Fixed costs}}{\text{Unit selling price} - \text{Variable costs per unit}}$$

This is quite logical. Before you can reach profits you must pay for the variable costs. This is done by deducting those costs from the unit selling price. What is left (usually called the unit contribution) is available to meet the fixed costs. Once enough units have been sold to meet these fixed costs, the BEP has been reached.

Let's try the sum out, given the following information shown on the break-even chart:

Fixed costs	=	£10,000
Selling price	=	£5 per unit
Variable cost	=	£3 per unit

$$\text{So BEP} = \frac{£10,000}{£5 - £3} = \frac{£10,000}{£2} = 5,000 \text{ units}$$

Now we can see that 5,000 units must be sold at £5 each before we can start to make a profit. We can also see that if 7,000 is our maximum output we have only 2,000 units available to make our required profit target.

Obviously, the more units we have available for sale (ie the maximum output that can realistically be sold) after our break-even point, the better. The relationship between total sales and the break-even point is called the margin of safety.

Margin of safety

This is usually expressed as a percentage and can be calculated as shown in Table 8.1.

Table 8.1 The calculation of a margin of safety

	£	
Total sales	35,000	(7,000 units × £5 selling price)
Minus break-even point	25,000	(5,000 units × £5 selling price)
Margin of safety	10,000	
Margin of safety as a percentage of sales	29%	(10,000 ÷ 35,000)

Clearly, the lower this percentage, the lower the business's capacity for generating profits. A low margin of safety might signal the need to rethink fixed costs, selling price or the maximum output of the business.

The angle formed at the BEP between the sales revenue line and the total costs line is called the angle of incidence. The size of the angle shows the rate at which profit is made after the break-even point. A large angle means a high rate of profit per unit sold after the BEP.

Costing to meet profit objectives

By adding in the final element, desired profits, we can have a comprehensive model to help us with costing and pricing decisions.

Supposing in the previous example we knew that we had to make £10,000 profits to achieve a satisfactory return on the capital invested in the business, we could amend out BEP formula to take account of this objective:

$$\text{BEPP (break-even profit point)} = \frac{\text{Fixed costs} + \text{Profit objective}}{\text{Unit selling price} - \text{Variable costs per unit}}$$

Putting some figures from our last example into this equation, and choosing £10,000 as our profit objective, we can see how it works.

$$\text{BEPP} = \frac{\pounds10{,}000 + \pounds10{,}000}{\pounds5 - \pounds3} = \frac{20{,}000}{2} = 10{,}000 \text{ units}$$

Unfortunately, without further investment in fixed costs, the maximum output in our example is only 7,000 units, so unless we change something the profit objective will not be met.

The great strength of this model is that each element can be changed in turn, on an experimental basis, to arrive at a satisfactory and achievable result.

Let us return to this example. We could start our experimenting by seeing what the selling price would have to be to meet our profit objective. In this case we leave the selling price as the unknown, but we have to decide the BEP in advance (you cannot solve a single equation with more than one unknown). It would not be unreasonable to say that we would be prepared to sell our total output to meet the profit objective.

So the equation now works out as follows:

$$7{,}000 = \frac{20{,}000}{\pounds\text{ Unit selling price} - \pounds3}$$

Moving the unknown over to the left-hand side of the equation we get:

$$\pounds\text{ Unit selling price} = \pounds3 + \frac{20{,}000}{7{,}000} = \pounds3 + 2.86 = \pounds5.86$$

We now know that with a maximum capacity of 7,000 units and a profit objective of £10,000, we have to sell at £5.86 per unit. Now if the market will stand that price, then this is a satisfactory result. If it will not, then we are back to experimenting with the other variables. We must find ways of decreasing the fixed or variable costs, or increasing the output of the plant, by an amount sufficient to meet our profit objective.

Costing for special orders

Every small business is laid open to the temptation of taking a particularly big order at a 'cut-throat' price. However attractive the proposition may look at first glance, certain conditions must be met before the order can be safely accepted.

Let us look at an example – a slight variation on the last one. Your company has a maximum output of 10,000 units, without any major investment in fixed costs. At present you are just not prepared to invest more money until the business has proved itself. The background information is:

Maximum output	10,000 units
Output to meet profit objective	7,000 units
Selling price	£5.86
Fixed costs	£10,000
Unit variable cost	£3.00
Profitability objective	£10,000

The break-even chart will look like Figure 8.6.

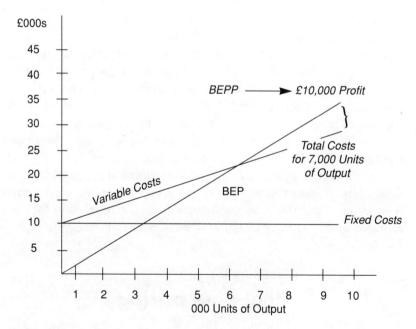

Figure 8.6   Break-even chart example

You are fairly confident that you can sell 7,000 units at £5.86 each, but that still leaves 3,000 units unsold – should you decide to produce them. Out of the blue an enquiry comes in for about 3,000 units, but you are given a strong hint that nothing less than a 33 per cent discount will clinch the deal. What should you do?

Using the costing information assembled so far, you can show the present breakdown of costs and arrive at your selling price.

Unit cost breakdown

	£	
Variable costs	3.00	
Contribution to fixed costs	1.43	(£10,000 fixed costs
		÷ 7,000 units)
Contribution to meet profitability objective	1.43	(£10,000 profitability objective ÷ 7,000 units)
Selling price	5.86	

As all fixed costs are met on the 7,000 units sold (or to be sold), the remaining units can be sold at a price that covers both variable costs and the profitability contribution, so you can negotiate at the same level of profitability, down to £4.43, just under 25 per cent off the current selling price. However, any selling price above the £3.00 variable cost will generate extra profits, but these sales will be at the expense of your profit margin. A lower profit margin in itself is not necessarily a bad thing if it results in a higher return on capital employed, but first you must do the sums (see Chapter 5).

There is a great danger with negotiating orders at marginal costs, as these costs are called, in that you do not achieve your break-even point soon enough and the deal results in a loss. (Look back to the first example in this chapter to see how missed sales targets affect profitability.)

Real-time pricing

With the advent of the Internet, a new type of 'special order' has been created. With accurate information on market demand, it is possible to vary prices infinitely to meet current demand exactly.

The stock market, for example, works by gathering information on supply and demand. If more people want to buy a share than to sell it, the price goes up until the amount of supply and demand are matched. If the information is perfect (when every buyer and seller knows what is going on), the price is optimised. For most businesses this is not a practical proposition. Their customers expect the same price every time for the same product or service. In any case, customers have no accurate idea what the demand is at any given moment in time.

For the Internet company, computer networks have made it possible to see how much consumer demand exists for a given product at any time. Anyone with a point-of-sale till could do the same, but the report may not come in until weeks later. This means that online companies could alter their prices hundreds of times a day, changing according to different circumstances or different markets, and so improve profits dramatically. EasyJet.com, a budget airline operating in Luton, does just this. It prices to fill its planes – you could pay anything from £30 to £200 for the same trip, depending on the demand for that flight.

However, alongside real-time pricing must come real-time break-even analyses. Unless you always know your position in relation to your break-even point, it is difficult to be certain that extra sales at lower prices will result in a greater profit.

Costing for business start-up

Paradoxically, one of the main reasons small businesses fail in the early stages is that too much start-up capital is used to buy fixed assets. While clearly some equipment is essential at the start, other purchases could be postponed. This may mean that 'desirable' and labour-saving devices have to be borrowed or hired for a specific period. Obviously this is not as nice as having them to hand all the time, but if, for example, photocopiers, computers, fax machines, scanners and even delivery vans are brought into the business, they become part of the fixed costs. The higher the fixed-cost plateau, the longer it usually takes to reach the break-even point and then profitability. And time is not usually on the side of the small new business. It has to become profitable relatively quickly or it will simply run out of money and die.

Look at these two hypothetical new small businesses. They are both making and selling identical products at the same price, £10. They plan to sell 10,000 units each in the first year. The owner of Company A plans to get fully equipped at the start. His fixed costs will be £40,000, double that of Company B. This is largely because, as well as his own car, he has bought such things as a delivery van, new equipment and a photocopier. Much of this will not be fully used for some time, but will save some money now. This extra expenditure will result in a lower unit variable cost than Company B can achieve, a typical capital intensive result (see Figure 8.7). Company B's owner, on the other hand, proposes to start up on a shoestring. Only £20,000 will go into fixed costs, but, of course, her unit variable cost will be higher, at £4.50. The variable cost is higher because, for example, she has to pay an outside carrier to deliver, while A uses his own van and pays only for petrol.

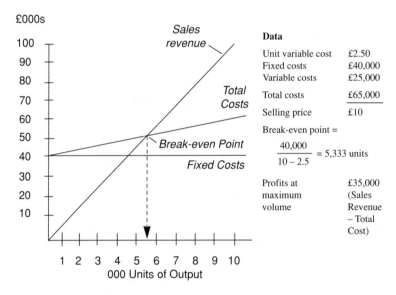

Figure 8.7 Break-even chart for Company A

The break-even chart for Company B is shown in Figure 8.8. From the data on each company you can see that total costs for 10,000 units are the same, so total possible profits, *if* 10,000 units are sold, are also the same. The key difference is that Company B starts making a profit after 3,636 units have been sold. Company A has to wait until 5,333 units have been sold.

Now another pair of reasons why small businesses fail very early on are connected with the marketplace. They are frequently over-optimistic on how much they can sell. They also underestimate how long it takes for sales to build up. So for these reasons, and spending too much start-up capital on fixed assets, great care should be taken to keep start-up fixed costs to the minimum.*

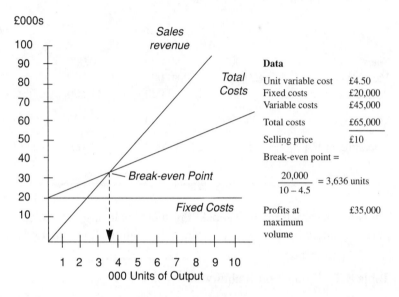

Figure 8.8   Break-even chart for Company B

Costing to eliminate unprofitable products

Not all the business's products will always be profitable. Settling down to allocate 'real' fixed costs to products can be something of an eye-opener to owner-managers. Look at the example below. The business

---

* There are all sorts of 'persuasive' arguments to go for a capital-intensive cost structure. In periods of high growth, the greater margin on sales will produce a higher ROCE, but high fixed costs will *always* expose a new or small business to higher risks. A small business has enough risks to face, with a survival rate of less than 20 per cent in its first few years, without adding to them.

manufactures three products. Product C is bulky, complicated and a comparatively slow seller. It uses all the same sorts of equipment, storage spare and sales effort as products A and B, only more so. When fixed costs are allocated across the range, it draws the greatest share (Table 8.2).

Table 8.2 Product profitability 1

	A	B	C	Total
	£	£	£	£
Sales	30,000	50,000	20,000	100,000
Variable costs	20,000	30,000	10,000	60,000
Allocated fixed costs	4,500	9,000	11,500	25,000
Total costs	24,500	39,000	21,500	85,000
Operating profit	5,500	11,000	(1,500)	15,000

This proves something of a shock. Product C is losing money, so it has to be eliminated, which will produce the situation shown in Table 8.3.

Table 8.3 Product profitability 2

	A	B	Total
	£	£	£
Sales	30,000	50,000	80,000
Variable costs	20,000	30,000	50,000
New allocated fixed costs	8,333	16,667	25,000
Total costs	28,333	46,667	75,000
Operating profit	1,667	3,333	5,000

Fixed costs will not change, so the £25,000 has to be re-allocated across the remaining two products. This will result in profits dropping from £15,000 to £5,000; therefore our conventional product costing system has given the wrong signals. We have lost all the 'contribution' that Product C made to fixed costs, and any product that makes a contribution will increase overall profits. Because fixed costs cannot be ignored, it makes more sense to monitor contribution levels and to allocate costs in proportion to them.

Looking back to Table 8.2, we can see that the products made the following contributions (Contribution = Sales – Variable costs) shown in Table 8.4.

Table 8.4 Allocating fixed costs by contribution level

		Contribution		Fixed cost allocated
		£	%	£
Product	A	10,000	25	6,250
	B	20,000	50	12,500
	C	10,000	25	6,250
Total		40,000	100	25,000

Now we can recast the product profit-and-loss account using this marginal costing basis (Table 8.5).

Table 8.5 Marginal costing product profit-and-loss account

	A	%	B	%	C	%	Total
	£		£		£		£
Sales	30,000		50,000		20,000		100,000
Marginal costs	20,000		30,000		10,000		60,000
Contribution	10,000	33	20,000	40	10,000	50	40,000
Fixed costs	6,250		12,500		6,250		25,000
Product profit	3,750	13	7,500	15	3,750	19	15,000

Not only should we not eliminate Product C, but because in contribution terms it is our most profitable product, we should probably try to sell more.

Questions

1. Calculate the margin of safety for Companies A and B in the example given on pages 138 and 139.
2. You are planning to start up a domestic burglar alarm business. You will be buying in the product and marketing it yourself. The main marketing effort will be a salesperson working on salary plus commission, and an advertising campaign. The financial facts are as follows (all expenses figures are for a four-month period):

Item	£
Car leasing charge	1,500
Sales commission, per unit	5
Salesperson's basic salary	5,000
Rent, rates, heat, light and power	3,500
Unit buy-in price	30
Other fixed costs	4,500
Unit installation cost	10
Advertising + literature	2,000
Sundry variable costs, per unit	5
Unit selling price	100

    (a) Calculate the break-even point.
    (b) You decide you must have £10,000 each half year to live off. Now what unit sales do you have to achieve?
    (c) You decide it is unrealistic to expect to sell more than 400 units in the first six months. What must your selling price be both to break even and to make the £10,000 you need to live off?
    (d) You decide to take on an installation engineer at £6,000 a half year together with another car on lease at £1,000 a half year. At the same time you increase the salesperson's salary to £8,000 and cancel the commission. Assuming that your unit selling price is once again £100, what are your answers to Questions (a), (b) and (c)?

Part 3

Business plans and budgets

9

Everyone has made a budget or plan at some time. In our personal lives we are always trying to match the scarce resource 'pay' with the ever-expanding range of necessities and luxuries in the market place, a battle we all too often lose, with mortgage costs, car running expenses, food and children's clothes taking more cash out than we can put in. Usually the domestic budget is confined to a periodic attempt to list and total likely future bills. These are then split into essential and non-essential items. The 'essential' total is then deducted from expected pay (or income) and if anything is left over we can plan how to spend it.

Temporary shortages of cash are made up by taking out an overdraft, the judicious use of a credit card, or talking to a rich aunt.

Every year we review how well we have kept within our budget and moan about the unexpected expenses that always knock us off course. The usual result is that next year's pay rise just about clears the overdraft in time to start again.

Budgeting for a business

A business has to do much the same type of budgeting and planning, although much more thoroughly if it wants to survive and prosper. A business's environment is much more complex than a individual's. For example, most people have only one main source of income, and the amount of money they are likely to get in any one year is fairly easy to predict accurately. Even the smallest business has dozens or even hundreds of potential sources of income – customers – but forecasting w much they will spend is not so easy. Some small businesses start off with their plans in the owner's head or on the back of the proverbial envelope. Most of these end up going broke in the first year. (There are simply not enough 'rich aunts' to go round.)

The central problem is that to make a profit a business must take risks. A small new business must take many more risks than an established or larger one, with each risk having more important consequences if things go wrong. For example, an established firm with a thousand customers can 'afford' to lose a few customers to the competition. A firm with a dozen customers cannot afford to lose any.

There is no way to eliminate all risks in business. Successful entrepreneurialism is all about anticipating the sort of risks that have to be taken, and understanding how they will affect the business. This knowledge is then used as the basis of a plan or budget. Putting this information together usually means gathering facts and opinions on the marketplace, interpreting their probable impact on your business, deciding what you want to happen, and finally deciding how you intend to make things happen; in other words, developing your strategy.

The small business that starts its life with a well-thought-through plan has great advantages over the 'seat of the pants' type of business. For a start, the plan or budget acts as a means of communicating your intentions to three vitally important audiences: the entrepreneur, the staff and the providers of finance. It is the entrepreneur's own 'dry run' before real money is put into the business and possibly lost. He or she can experiment with various sales levels, profit margins and growth rates to arrive at a realistic picture of how he or she would like the business to develop, before committing himself to a particular course of action. We looked at a variation of this approach in Chapter 8 when we examined the relationship between cost/volume/profit and prices. This process will give the entrepreneur an invaluable insight into the mechanics of the business and help him or her to prepare for problems before they happen.

Also, other people working in the business will be in a better position to pull together if they know where the business is going. They can then become committed to common goals and strategies.

Bankers or shareholders outside the business will be more likely to be supportive if they see that the owner-manager knows what he or she wants to happen, and how to make it come about. For example, they will not be surprised by calls for cash to finance sales growth, or capital expenditure if they have seen the plans in advance.

Finally, most people who start up in business are fairly competitive. The budget acts as a standard against which they can measure their own business performance. This is particularly important for a new business in its first trading period, with no history to go on. In other words you cannot really try to do better than last year if there wasn't one, so the only guide available is a realistic and achievable plan.

Timescale and detail

Any attempt at planning invariably begs the question 'How far ahead should I plan?' The answer 'As far ahead as you can usefully see' is not particularly helpful, but it is the one most frequently given. Here are a few guidelines that may help bring the planning horizon into view.

Outsiders, such as bankers, may have a standard period over which they expect you to plan, if you want to borrow money from them. Usually this is at least three years, and for a new business preparing its first plan, three years is probably at the horizon itself.

The *payback period*, discussed in Chapter 7, is another useful concept. If it is going to take you four or five years to recover your original investment and make a satisfactory profit, then that is how far you may want to plan.

The *rate of technological change* is yet another yardstick used in deciding how far ahead to plan. If your business is high-tech or substantially influenced by changes in technology, then that factor must influence your choice of planning horizon. Companies in the early stages of the computer business who looked only three years ahead would have missed all the crucial technological trends, and as technological trends are vital factors influencing the success of any business in this field, the planning time horizon must accommodate them.

The amount of detail with which you plan may also help to make a long planning horizon more feasible. For example, every business should plan its first year in considerable detail. As well as a description of what the business is going to do, these plans should be summarised into a month-by-month cash-flow projection;* a comprehensive quarterly profit-and-loss account; and a full opening and closing position balance sheet. This first-year plan is usually called the *budget*.

---

*In a cash business such as a shop you need to project cash flow on a weekly basis.

Future years could be planned in rather less detail, giving only quarterly cash-flow projection, for example. If the planning horizon is very
long, plans for the final years could be confined to statements about
market (and technological) trends, anticipated market share and profit
margins. The detail of these plans is covered more comprehensively
later in this chapter.

One final point before we look at how the budget and plans are
prepared. There is a tendency to think of the budgeting process as a
purely financial exercise, rather theoretical and remote from the day-
to-day activity of the business. This is a serious misconception, usually
fostered in larger companies, where the planners and the doers lead
separate existences. People who have spent time in a large organisation
have to recognise that in a small business the decision maker has to
prepare his or her own planning. No one likes to have someone else's
plans foisted upon him or her, a useful point to remember if a small
business has a number of decision takers working in it.

In the end the budgets and plans are expressed in financial terms:
cash-flow forecasts, profit-and-loss accounts and balance sheets. But
the process of preparing the budget is firmly rooted in the real business
world.

Objectives

'To the man who does not know where he is going – any road will take
him there.' Every plan needs to start with a clear objective if it is to
succeed. At the simplest level, for example, imagine you are planing a
journey. Before you can consider whether to fly, drive, walk or take a
train, you have to know your destination. You also have to know when
you want to arrive and how much baggage you need with you. In other
words, a clear objective. 'I want to be in Edinburgh on Thursday not
later than 11 am with no more than an overnight bag.' This is a clear,
unambiguous objective and only now can you plan the route and the
means of transport in the most effective manner.

A business also needs clear objectives to be stated before the
budgeting and planning process can get under way. It needs both
market and financial objectives to cover the range of its activities.

Market objectives

Sometimes referred to as the business mission or purpose, market objectives go beyond a simple statement of what product(s) you are going to sell. This mission should define precisely the market you are entering and in a way that helps you to understand the needs you are trying to satisfy. To some extent products come and go, but markets go on forever – at least the needs that the products aim to satisfy do. A simple reflection on the way in which people satisfy the need to travel will illustrate the transient nature of products. While the need to travel has grown rapidly over the past 50 years, with more people travelling more often, 'products' such as the railways and ocean liners have declined. New 'products', the motor car, the coach and the aeroplane have absorbed all the extra demand and more. (It goes without saying that this market must be compatible with your own skills and resources. A fundamental mismatch in this area would be fatal.)

For example, you may be skilled at designing and making clothes. The marketplace could be vast. You could concentrate on high fashion, one-off dresses, perhaps produce a range of inexpensive clothes for young girls, or you could make and market baby clothes. Each of these markets is different, and until you define your 'mission' you cannot start to plan. The following statement is the mission of one small business: 'We will design, make and market clothes for mothers-to-be that make them feel they can still be fashionably dressed'. This meets the two criteria every mission must meet.

First, it is narrow enough to give direction and guidance to everyone in the business. This concentration is the key to business success, because it is only by focusing on specific needs that a small business can differentiate itself from its larger competitors. Nothing kills off new business faster than trying to do too many different things too quickly. But the mission narrows down the task in clear steps: we are concentrating on women; this is further reduced to women at a certain stage in their lives, ie pregnancy; this is finally reduced to those pregnant women who are fashion conscious. This is a clearly recognised need which specific products can be produced to satisfy. This is also a well-defined market that we can come to grips with.

Second, the example mission opens up a large market to allow the business to grow and realise its potential.

Interestingly enough, one of the highest incidences of failure in small businesses is in the building trade. The very nature of this field seems to mitigate against being able to concentrate on any specific type of work, or customer need. One successful new small builder defined his mission in the following sentence. 'We are going to concentrate on domestic house repair and renovation work, and as well as doing a good job we will meet the customer's two key needs: a quotation that is accurate and starting and completion dates that are met.' When told this mission, most small builders laugh. They say it cannot be done, but then most go broke.

At the end of the day, there has to be something unique about your business idea or yourself that makes people want to buy from you. That uniqueness may be confined to the fact that you are the only photocopying shop in the area, but that is enough to make you stand out (provided of course that the area has potential customers).

Also, within the market objective area you need some idea of how big you want the business to be. Your share of the market, in other words. It certainly is not easy to forecast sales, especially before you have even started trading, but if you do not set a goal at the start and you just wait and see how things develop, then one of two problems will occur. Either you will not sell enough to cover your fixed costs and you will lose money and perhaps go out of business. Or you will sell too much and run out of cash, ie overtrade (see Chapter 3).

Obviously, before you can set a market share and sales objective you need to know the size of your market. We shall consider how to find that out in the next section of this chapter. Later on, when the business has been trading for a few years, it may be possible to use that sales history and experience to forecast ahead. If there are few customers, then you can build up likely sales on a customer-by-customer basis. If there are many, then some simple mathematical technique, perhaps computer based, could be used.

But to a large extent the 'size' you want your business to be is more a judgement than a forecast, a judgement tempered by the resources you have available to achieve those objectives and, of course, some idea of what is reasonable and achievable and what is not. You will find the range of discretion over a size objective seriously constrained by the financial objectives chosen.

Profit objectives

The profit objective of every business must be to make a satisfactory return on the capital employed. We saw in Chapter 4, on business controls, that unless the return on capital employed ratio was at a certain level, a business would find it very difficult to attract outside funds. A bank manager would be fairly cool to a request for a long-term loan well below market rates. By definition 'market rates' means he or she could lend the money elsewhere at a satisfactory rate.

Another yardstick might be how much profit other people make in this type of business, even how much you could make if you invested elsewhere.

As well as making a satisfactory ROCE, the business and its profits have to grow, otherwise it will not earn enough to replace equipment or launch new products, both costly exercises. And without working equipment and a fresh product range to match the competition a business is effectively dead or dying.

So the main objectives of a new business with, say, £50,000 start-up capital, that wanted to double sales in four years, grow a little faster than the market, make a healthy and growing ROCE, and increase slightly its profit margin, might be summarised as follows:

Table 9.1 Business objectives

	Start-up budget	Planning period	4 years on
Sales	£80,000	Details	£160,000
Profit margin	12.5%	omitted	13.5%
Profit	£10,000		£21,600
Capital employed	£50,000		£86,400
ROCE	20%		25%
Market share	5%		7%

Without a well-defined mission and clearly stated objectives a business leaves its success to chance and improvisation. (Chance leads most small businesses to fail in their first three years.)

Once we have set these primary objectives, the purpose of the budget and plans is to make sure we can achieve them. Stating the objectives provides a clear guide to future action. For example, it is obvious from the primary objectives on ROCE and profit margins that an extra £36,400 (£86,400–£50,000) of capital is needed to finance the desired sales growth over the period of the plan.

There is a school of thought that says you have to build up your plans from and appreciation of markets and resource, as described below. Then an objective can be deduced as the sum of the achievable tasks. But this exposes you to the question 'What if this sum is not satisfactory?' It could also leave opportunity untapped. Neither of these is a very satisfactory position, so the objective's first approach, and then market appreciation, must be adopted.

Market appreciation

All businesses live or die by virtue of their success or otherwise in the marketplace. People very often talk of a particular market or business sector as being profitable, but without much idea of why. Years of research into the factors that influence a market's relative profitability have produced the following conclusion. 'The more intense the competition, the lower the return on capital employed.' While that does not come as a great surprise in itself, it does provide some valuable pointers on how to analyse the marketplace. It follows that any budget or plan must be based on a sound appreciation of the competitive forces at work in a market, otherwise the primary profit objective may simply not be attainable.

For someone who has not yet started up a business, this process can act as a filter to eliminate the undesirable. For those already trading, it can provide guidance on areas upon which to concentrate and on likely problem areas.

Figure 9.1 shows a way to look at these competitive forces as a whole.

Before you can start to plan in any detail you need answers to the following questions:

- *Where is my market?* The starting point in any market appreciation has to be a definition of the scope of the market you are aiming for. A small general shop may only serve the needs of a few dozen streets. A specialist restaurant may have to call on a catchment area of 10 or 20 miles. While trends and behaviour in the wider market are helpful facts to know, your main activity is within your own area.

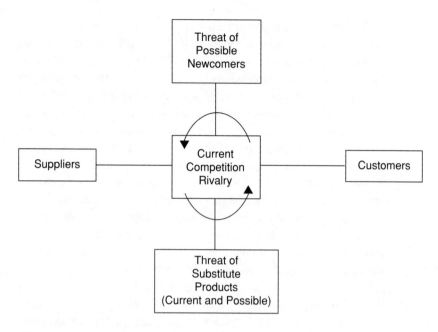

Figure 9.1   Competitive forces in a market

You may eventually decide to sell to several different markets. For example, a retail business can serve a local area through its shop and a national area by mail order. A small manufacturing business can branch out into exporting. People all too often flounder in their market research by describing their markets too broadly; for example, the motor industry, when they really mean car sales in Perth, or health foods, when they mean wholemeal bread in one small village.

● *Who are the customers, potential and actual?* Some products are aimed at the general public, others at particular trades or professions, males or females only, or perhaps large institutions and government departments. Some products cut across all these customer groups.

Focusing on the particular people who could buy the product gives a better idea of how many are likely to buy. Equally important, it will help you understand why they should buy from you. This really is the key to the whole business and its growth.

One entrepreneur started up a drinks vending machine business. Finding a vending machine that was reliable and easy to operate and maintain was the first task he tackled. This took two months. Next he searched for suitable ingredients, ending up with a very acceptable and economic range of hot and cold drinks. He then found a finance company to lease machines to his customers. All this vital background work took nearly four months and eventually he hit the road selling. He quickly found that his potential customers were new or smallish businesses without a vending machine already, most of which were unacceptable to the leasing company because they had no financial track record. Or he had to find a large company that was on the point of changing its equipment for one reason or another. The nature of his potential customers meant he had to call cold. (An advertising campaign using leaflets would take a long time to produce sales and he had already spent half his working capital.) He had to make something like 80 cold calls to get two interviews and it took 10 interviews to get three quotations in. Only one of those would result in an order. He ran out of cash before he could get a significant number of customers, as well as having a nervous breakdown from cold calling, a task he did not enjoy. Bringing his potential customers sharply into focus at the start and taking account of them in his business plan might have avoided this disaster.

- *How big is the market?* You need to know this to see whether or not your sales objectives are reasonable and attainable. If there are only 1,000 possible customers for your product in the geographical market you have chosen, and five well-established competitors, then expecting to sell to 500 of them in year 1 is not on.

- *Is the market growing or contracting?* In a growth market there are often opportunities for new companies to come in, or for small businesses to expand. In a contracting market existing competitors slog it out, leaving little room for new entrants or expansion. You should find out in which direction the market is moving and at what speed. The state of the general economy may not have much bearing on the market you are in. For example, the number of video rental outlets reached their zenith in a period of economic decline in the UK.

● *Who are the competition and what are their strengths and weaknesses?* Most products have competitors. To some extent this is reassuring because you know in advance that you are likely to achieve some sales, but you have to identify who they are and how they can affect your business. You have to know everything about them: their product range, prices, discount structure, delivery arrangements, specifications, minimum order quantities, terms of trade, etc.

  You also have to look at two less visible types of competitor. First, those who have not yet arrived on the scene. You have to consider what conditions would attract new businesses into the market. For example, businesses that require very little start-up capital, or add little value to goods, are always vulnerable to new competitors opening up. On the other hand, a business that can protect its ideas with patents, or achieve high-volume sales quickly, is less exposed. Second, under certain circumstances customers can be persuaded to buy a quite different or substitute product from the one you are offering, and still satisfy their same needs. In other words, you have a secondary layer of competition.

● *Who are the suppliers?* Most businesses buy in and process raw materials of one sort or another. They add value, sell out, and make a profit. If you have only a handful of possible suppliers, then they have the initiative and can set the terms of trade. For a new small business the problem is very often one of finding someone to supply in small enough volume. Nevertheless, it is a key strategic task to find at least two sources of supply for all vital products, and to negotiate the best possible deal. Otherwise the products themselves will be uncompetitive.

Forecasting sales

One of our primary market objectives is how much we would like to sell – or need to sell to achieve profit objectives. For a new business this and market share may be the only guidelines as to what sales volume could be achieved. The new business could also see what other similar ventures had achieved in their early years. However, a business with a sales history has another clue – the sales trend.

Figure 9.2 shows the quarterly sales results of a hypothetical business that has been trading for the past two years. Sales have grown from about 50 units per quarter up to just over 200 in the eight quarters.

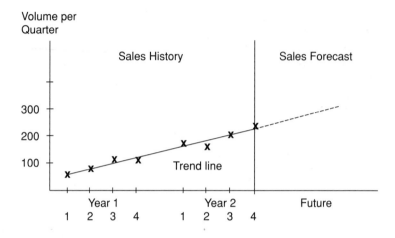

Figure 9.2   Graph showing sales trend

It is possible, either mathematically or by eye, to fit a trend line through these points. Continuing this trend line over the planning period shows what sales are likely to be, if the past can be accepted as a good guide to the future.

Now we can superimpose our sales objective on to a chart showing the sales trend. This will show the gap between where the business is going by virtue of its own momentum, and where we should like sales to be (see Figure 9.3).

Apart from continuing our present efforts to achieve sales and sales growth, our objectives call for extra results to fill the sales gap, so within our sales operating plan specific tasks to achieve this growth have to be identified.

It is beyond the scope of this book to give more than an outline of the task involved in a market appreciation suitable for preparing a business plan. While most financial matters are common to all types of enterprise, most marketing matters are unique to a particular business.

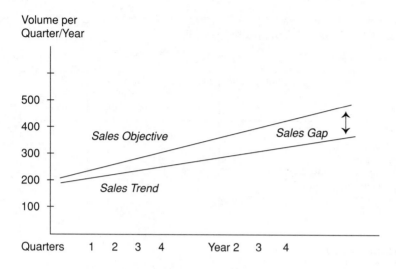

Figure 9.3 Gap analysis

Resources appreciation

Market appreciation is a look outside the business to see the opportunities and threats to the business and its products. A business reacts to these by mobilising its resources to take advantage of the opportunities and to neutralise the threats. Business resources can be loosely grouped under four main headings: people, facilities, information and finance.

People

People are vital to the success or failure of the business. Before you begin to identify specific people it is probably more important to highlight the sorts of skills and knowledge you want them to have. So the process could be summarised as a series of questions with the answers giving some guidance for future action.

Auditing your own knowledge and skills is an obvious starting point. By identifying gaps in these you can decide whom you need. The worksheet on page 158 will help to get ideas flowing.

You can then search out other people or agencies that you need to help achieve your objectives.

Figure 9.4 Personal skills resource audit

How good are you at:

	Satisfactory	Inadequate	Person/ help available	If not, what will you do?

MARKETING
  Market research
  Salesmanship
  Publicity/advertising
  Product development
  Distribution
  Others (list)				

PRODUCTION
  Technical matters
  Buying
  Planning production
  Quality control
  Stock control
  Others (list)				

PEOPLE
  Selecting people
  Leading people
  Motivating people
  Teamwork
  Listening to people
  Giving clear
    instructions
  Others (list)				

FINANCE AND
ADMINISTRATION
  Forming a company
    or partnership
  Finding premises
  Bookkeeping, tax and
    and VAT
  Raising money
  Budgeting and
    managing money
  Collecting in money
  Writing letters
  Forward planning
  Dealing with
    regulations
  Others (list)				

Facilities audit

Facilities, such as an office, workshop space, storage, machinery, etc, are another key resource. The worksheet below can summarise the position here.

1. What fixtures, fittings, premises, etc do you have or need? List.

Need	Have	Can borrow	Must find

2. What production equipment, etc do you have or need? List.

Need (including some idea of output that can be achieved)	Have	Can borrow	Must find

3. Other key facilities.

You may find you already have resources you do not need. You should either put them to use or dispose of them if they cannot be pressed into service soon. They will only increase the fixed-asset base of the business, tie up capital unnecessarily and make it harder to achieve your ROCE objective. (Look back at Chapter 5 to refresh your memory.)

Information audit

Information, other than pure market information, is also an important and frequently neglected resource area. Carry out an information audit.

1. What bookkeeping system have you planned? Who will run it and will it give you the control you need?
2. Are there any possible legal problems related to:
   - your product or service;
   - your premises;
   - present or future employees;
   - yourself (ie conditions in a past service contract may prevent you from working in a certain field);
   - patents, etc?

Financial resources audit

Financial resources are clearly an important consideration in any planning process. They are nearly always the major constraint in any plans for a new business, whether starting up or expanding. A financial resources audit looks for answers to three questions. How much money have you got that you are prepared to commit to your business? How much do you need? Where will you get the balance from?

1. Obviously the first thing to do is to find out exactly how much you have to invest in the business. You may not have much in ready cash, but you may have valuable assets that can be converted into cash, or other borrowing. The difference between your assets and liabilities is your 'net worth'. This is the maximum security that you can offer for any money borrowed, and it is to be hoped that the calculations in Table 9.3 will yield a pleasant surprise.

Table 9.2 Your net worth

Liabilities	£	Assets	£
Overdraft		Cash in hand and in banks,	
Mortgage		building societies, National Savings	
Other loans		or other deposits	
Hire purchase		Stocks and shares	
Tax due,		Current redemption value of	
including		insurance policies	
Capital Gains		Value of home	
Credit cards due		Any other property	
Garage, local		Motor car(s), etc	
shop accounts		Jewellery, paintings and other	
due		marketable valuables	
Any other		Any money due to you	
financial		Value of your existing business	
obligations			
Total liabilities		Total assets	

Net worth = Total assets – Total liabilities

2. The sum you need to achieve your plan is calculated as follows:
   (a) First-year start-up costs: £
       Fixed capital (tools, equipment, premises, etc)
       Working capital (materials, opening stocks,
           wages, rent, your living expenses, etc)

       Total start-up costs

   (b) Additional capital to finance growth. (In Table 9.1, item 4,
       the additional capital required is £36,400.)
   (c) Total capital required over planning period is the total of (a)
       and (b).
3. The capital you need to find is the amount by which 2 exceeds 1.

Key strategies and operating plans

So far in the budgeting and planning process we have set our business objectives, looked at market opportunities and examined our own resources. The next step is to decide what resources to commit to what market and business tasks.

Key strategies are areas of action that are vital to the success of the business. The market strategies define exactly what products/services you plan to offer to which specific customer group(s). The financial strategies explain the sources of funds and the profitability expected.

An *operating plan* must be made for each area of the business. For example, sales, advertising, production, equipment purchasing, raw material supplies, premises, deliveries, etc. The operating plan must state the specific task to be achieved and when; what will be done, by whom, and by what date. It should also monitor results. If appropriate, each task should also have an expense budget estimate against it. Your plans are complete when you have set enough tasks to achieve your primary business objectives. These plans must not be complicated, but they must be written down. They provide the backbone to the business, and the statement for others (bankers, shareholders, etc) to see that you know your business direction.

An example of an operating plan is shown in Table 9.3 on page 163.

People launching small businesses or trying to expand never cease to be amazed at how long their plans take to come to fruition. The much quoted rule is to estimate a timescale, double it, then double it again for good measure. The problem is that most of them simply do not think through their plans step by step, in the manner prescribed for an operating plan. Small businesses simply do not have the cash resources to allow for extensive timescales.

Contingency plans

Any plan is built on a number of assumptions. Many of these assumptions are outside the planner's control, and some are keys to the success of the venture. Look back at the earlier example of a personal objective to get to Edinburgh by a certain time (page 148). Suppose, after reviewing all the market opportunities (ie trains, planes, hire cars, buses, etc) and assessing our resources (ie money, our own car, etc), we

Table 9.3 Example of an operating plan

Operating plan, year_____

Planning area	Task/objective	Cost budget	Timescale	Action required	Date	By whom	Results of task on costs
Premises	Find 2,000 sq ft of warehouse space within five miles of workshop	£800	April–July (must be in and working by 1 August)	1. Look at area.	6/5	GFK	
				2. Contact estate agents a, b, c.	6/5	GFK	
				3. Search papers.	10/5	GFK	
				4. Visit possible sites.	10/6	GFK	
				5. Review leases.	20/6	TRD	
				6. Sign up.	1/7	TRD	
				7. Take over premises.	20/7	GFK	
Raw material suppliers	Find two competitive suppliers of raw material 'x'	Petty cash	April–June	1. Search trade journals.	6/5	TJ	
				2. Write for specification and quotes.	10/5	TJ	
				3. Chase up replies.	15/5	TJ	
				4. Visit four best possibles.	20/5	TJ	
				5. Place trial orders.	25/5	TRD	
				6. Select two best.	15/6	TRD	
				7. Place orders.	25/6	TJ	

decide to go by train. Unfortunately, when we get to the station we find the train has been cancelled.

A key assumption in our plan is that the train will run – but this is clearly outside our control. If by going for the train, we miss the opportunity to fly, and it is then too late to go by car or bus, we have no contingency plans; no means of achieving our objective. Now obviously in this example we could postpone going to Edinburgh, or perhaps arrive later after telephoning to explain.

But there are business situations where our objectives must be met on time, and viable contingency plans have to be prepared to make sure this happens.

For example, if a piece of production equipment breaks down, do you know where you can hire or borrow a spare quickly? Small businesses cannot afford to be out of commission for long, so contingency arrangements for all sensitive areas are essential.

Setting the budget

Only now is it possible to construct a detailed financial picture of a business's budget and plans. The budget sets out, line by line in much the same format as the profit-and-loss account, the major sources of income and expenditure for the period of the budget. The year is broken down into weeks or months, depending on the dynamics of the business.

The best way to budget is to look one year ahead and review the whole budget each quarter. At that review, add a further quarter to the forecast so that you always have a one-year budget horizon. This is known as a 'rolling quarterly budget'. It may seem like hard work at first, but the sooner budgeting becomes a regular business routine rather than an annual chore, the more accurate your forecasts will become. This not only makes the whole planning process both easier and more reliable, but it can also have the knock-on effect of making your business more creditworthy and valuable. Any business that consistently meets or exceeds its targets will have its profit targets accepted more readily than one with a patchy performance in relation to its targets.

Budget guidelines

- The budget must be based on realistic but *challenging* goals. Those goals are arrived at by both a top-down 'aspiration' and a bottom-up forecast of what seems both possible and likely. For example, if sales have been growing at a rate of 10 per cent a year for the past couple of years, a 10 per cent increase in sales seems a 'possible and likely' outcome for next year – a target that your sales force might be expected to aim for. However, your business plan may involve an attempt to grow at a faster rate than in the past. In this case, a goal of 15 per cent would be acceptable – challenging, but realistic.
- The budget should be prepared by those responsible for delivering the results – the salespeople should prepare the sales budget and the production people the production budget. You need to manage the communication process so that everyone knows what other parties are planning for.
- Agreement to the budget should be explicit. During the budgeting process, several versions of a particular budget should be discussed. For example, the boss may want a sales figure of £2 million, but the sales team's initial forecast is for £1.75 million. After some debate, £1.9 million may be the figure agreed upon. Once a figure is agreed, a virtual contract exists that declares a commitment from employees to achieve the target and commitments from the employer to be satisfied with the target and to supply resources in order to achieve it. It makes sense for this contract to be in writing.
- The budget needs to be finalised at least a month before the start of the year and not weeks or months into the year. The sooner people know their goals, the sooner they can start to achieve them.
- The budget should undergo fundamental reviews periodically throughout the year to make sure all the basic assumptions that underpin it still hold good. For example, the market itself may be growing much faster than you expected, so rendering your goals too easy to achieve.
- You need up-to-date and accurate information to make the process worthwhile. Figures should be ready for review 7 to 10 working days before the month's end.

Monitoring performance

Performance needs to be carefully monitored and compared against the budget as the year proceeds, and corrective action must be taken where necessary to keep the two consistent. This has to be done on a monthly basis (or using shorter time intervals if required), showing both the company's performance during the month in question and throughout the year so far.

Table 9.4 The fixed budget

Heading	Month			Year to date		
	Budget	Actual	Variance	Budget	Actual	Variance
Sales	805*	753	(52)	6,358	7,314	956
Materials	627	567	60	4,942	5,704	(762)
Materials margin	178	186	8	1,416	1,610	194
Direct costs	74	79	(5)	595	689	(94)
Gross profit	104	107	3	820	921	101
Percentage	**12.92**	**14.21**	**1.29**	**12.90**	**12.60**	**(0.30)**

* Figures indicate thousands of pounds

Looking at Table 9.4, we can see at a glance that the business is behind on sales for this month, but ahead on the yearly target. The convention is to put all unfavourable variations in brackets. Hence, a higher-than-budgeted sales figure does not have brackets, whilst a higher materials cost does. We can also see that, whilst profit is running ahead of budget, the profit margin is slightly behind (–0.30 per cent). This is partly because other direct costs, such as labour and distribution in this example, are running well ahead of budget.

Flexing the budget

A budget is based on a particular set of sales goals, few of which are likely to be exactly met in practice.

Table 9.4 shows a company that has used £762,000 more materials than budgeted. As more has been sold, this is hardly surprising. The way to manage this situation is to flex the budget to show what, given the sales that actually occurred, would be expected to happen to expenses. This is done by applying the budget ratios to the actual data. For example, materials were planned to be 22.11 per cent of sales in the budget. By applying that to the actual month's sales, a materials cost of £587,000 is arrived at.

Looking at the flexed budget in Table 9.5, we can see that the company has spent £19,000 more than expected on the material given the level of sales actually achieved, rather than the £762,000 overspend shown in the fixed budget.

Table 9.5 The flexed budget

Heading	Month			Year to date		
	Budget	Actual	Variance	Budget	Actual	Variance
Sales	753*	753	–	7,314	7,314	–
Materials	587	567	20	5,685	5,704	(19)
Materials margin	166	186	20	1,629	1,610	(19)
Direct costs	69	79	(10)	685	689	(4)
Gross profit	97	107	10	944	921	(23)
Percentage	**12.92**	**14.21**	**1.29**	**12.90**	**12.60**	**(0.30)**

* Figures indicate thousands of pounds

The same principle holds for other direct costs, which appear to be running £94,000 over budget for the year. When we take into account the extra sales shown in the flexed budget, we can see that the company has actually spent £4,000 over budget on direct costs. Whilst this is serious, it is not as serious as the fixed budget suggests.

The flexed budget allows you to concentrate your efforts on dealing with true variances in performance.

Seasonality and trends

The figures shown for each period of the budget are not the same. For example, a sales budget of £1.2 million for the year does not translate to £100,000 a month. The exact figure depends on two factors. The projected trend may forecast that, while sales at the start of the year are £80,000 a month, they will change to £120,000 a month by the end of the year. The average would be £100,000.

By virtue of seasonal factors, each month may also be adjusted up or down from the underlying trend. You could expect the sales of heating oil, for example, to peak in the autumn and tail off in the late spring. Figure 9.5 suggests what this might look like when displayed on a chart.

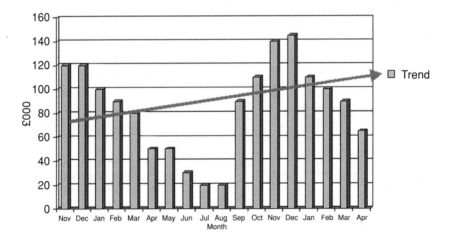

Figure 9.5   Seasonal budget showing trend

Cash and capital budgets

The budget will not just have implications on profit and loss. If sales goals are high, there may be a requirement for more equipment to produce the product. This would have capital implications as more funds may have to found.

Also, there may be implications on cash flow. Rapidly increasing the number of sales of manufactured products necessitates spending large

amounts of cash on raw materials and labour and fi
until they pay up. As long as sales growth accelei
increases. This is not necessarily harmful, but it must b
by preparing a cash-flow forecast based on the budget.

Building a budget model

Setting a budget requires discussion with key staff – several different
sets of figures may have to be produced. A budget model built using a
spreadsheet is the ideal way to compile these. By using spreadsheets,
the effect on the budget of changing any figure or figures can be seen
automatically and instantly without any tedious calculations. All that is
required is for someone to decide the relationship between the various
elements of the budget – for example, that debtors will be given 45
days to pay, or that the gross margin should be 50 per cent. Thereafter,
changes in sales levels as the budget is formulated will just 'roll down'
the model to produce revised profit-and-loss accounts and balance
sheets.

A further advantage of going for a computerised bookkeeping
system is that it has a budgeting model framework built in. The model
is also useful for budget updates and revisions throughout the year.

10 *Writing and presenting business plans*

For most entrepreneurs, the principal reason for writing up a business plan is to persuade someone to fund or partially fund their venture.

It follows, therefore, that you must give some thought as to the needs of prospective investors, and to explain how these can be accommodated when writing up and presenting your business plan.

What financiers look out for

All successful businesses need finance at some stage in their development, so, as well as preparing a business plan to reap operational benefits, it is important to examine what financiers expect from you if you want to succeed in raising those funds.

It is often said that there is no shortage of money for new and growing businesses – the only scarce commodities are good ideas and people with the ability to exploit them. From the potential entrepreneur's position this is often hard to believe. Out of every 1,000 business plans received by venture-capital providers, only 100 or so are examined in any detail, less than 10 are pursued to the negotiating stage and only 1 is invested in.

To a great extent, the decision whether or not to proceed beyond an initial reading of a plan depends on the quality of the financial arguments contained within it and the revenue model used to support the investment proposal. The business plan is the 'ticket of admission' that gives entrepreneurs their first – and often only – chance to impress prospective sources of finance with the quality of their proposal.

It follows from this that, to have any chance at all of getting financial support, a business plan must consider the likely requirements of potential financiers.

Bankers, and indeed any other sources of debt capital, are looking for asset security to back their loan and the near certainty of getting their money back. Essentially, banks are in the business of converting illiquid assets, such as property or stock, into liquid assets such as cash or overdraft facilities. They will charge an interest rate that reflects current market conditions and their view of the level of risk involved in the proposal. Depending on the nature of the business in question and the purpose to which the money is being used, bankers will use a two- to five-year forecast.

Bankers usually expect a business to start repaying both the loan and the interest on a monthly or quarterly basis immediately after the loan has been granted. In some cases a capital holiday of up to two years can be negotiated, but in the early stages of any loan the interest charges make up the lion's share of payments, like mortgage repayments. You need to allow for this in your cash-flow projections.

Bankers hope that a business will succeed so that they can lend more money in the future and provide more banking services, such as insurance or tax advice to loyal customers.

It follows from this appreciation of lenders' needs that they are less interested in rapid growth and the consequent capital gain than they are in a steady stream of earnings almost from the outset.

As most new or fast-growing businesses do not generally make immediate profits, money for such enterprises must come from elsewhere. Risk or equity capital, as other types of funds are called, comes from venture-capital houses, or is contributed by the founders of the company, their families and/or their friends.

Because the risks of investing in new and young ventures are greater than those of investing in established companies, venture-capital fund managers have to offer their investors the chance of larger overall returns. To do that, fund managers must not only keep failures to a minimum, they have to pick some big winners too – ventures with annual compound growth rates above 35 per cent – to offset the inevitable mediocre performers. With this in mind it is hardly surprising that the new economy has sucked in so much equity finance. Out of ten investments made, a fund manager would typically expect one star, seven also-rans and two flops. However, it is important to remember that, despite the fallibility of their choices, venture-capital fund managers are only looking for winners, so unless you are projecting high growth, the chances of getting venture capital are slim.

Not only are venture capitalists looking for winners, they are also looking for substantial shareholdings in the businesses in which they invest. There are no simple rules as to what constitutes a fair split of the business. However, as a rough rule of thumb, these suggestions offer some guidance:

- for the idea: 33 per cent;
- for the management: 33 per cent;
- for the money: 33 per cent.

If a venture-capital firm sees that you have a great idea and a first-class team, it may aim for a third of your business as its reward for putting up the money. If your team is weak, it may want to put in a non-executive director and work with you to strengthen the team. For this, they may aim for more than a third of your business in return for their investment.

It all comes down to how much you need the money, how risky the venture is, how much money could be made, and your skills as a negotiator. However, it is salutary to remember that 100 per cent of nothing is still nothing, so all parties to the deal have to be satisfied if it is to succeed.

As fast-growing companies typically have no cash available to pay dividends and, as is the case of many e-businesses, may not have made any profits yet, investors can only profit by selling their holdings. With this in mind, the venture capitalists need to have an 'exit route', such as the stock exchange or a potential corporate buyer, in view at the outset.

Unlike many entrepreneurs (and some lending bankers) who see their ventures as lifelong commitments to success and growth, venture capitalists have a relatively short-term horizon. Typically, they are looking to liquidate small-company investments within two to six years, allowing them to pay out individual investors and to have funds available for the winners of the future. Your financial plan needs to recognise this timescale.

To be successful, your business must be targeted at the needs of these two sources of finance, and in particular at the proportions invested by them. Lending bankers ideally look for a ratio of 1:1, which means that half the businesss finances are borrowed and half comes from risk capital. Banks have been known to go to 4:1, contributing four times more than risk-capital sources, but rarely do this willingly or at the outset of their involvement. Venture-capital providers will almost always encourage entrepreneurs to take on new debt capital to match the level of equity funding. If you are planning to raise money from friends and relatives either as debt or equity, then their needs must also be taken account of in your business plan.

Entrepreneurs are naturally ebullient when explaining the future prospects of their businesses. They frequently believe that 'the sky's the limit' when it comes to growth, and that money (or rather, a lack of it) is the only thing that stands between them and their success.

Whilst it is true that if you are looking for venture capital, the providers are looking for rapid growth, remember that financiers are dealing with thousands of investment proposals every year and already have money tied up in hundreds of business sectors. It follows, therefore, that they already have a perception of what the accepted financial results and marketing approaches currently are within different sectors. Any new company's business plan showing projections that are outside the ranges perceived as acceptable within an industry will raise questions in the investor's mind.

Make your growth forecasts *believable*; support them with hard facts where possible. If they are on the low side, then approach the more cautious lending banker rather than venture capitalists. The former often see a modest forecast as a virtue, which lends credibility to the business proposal as a whole.

Appearance and size

The most important purpose of any written material is to create a favourable first impression. Financiers seem to have common views as to what constitutes a potentially winning business plan proposal:

● In general, they want the appearance to look workmanlike. In other words, not a leatherbound book or a series of odd pages cobbled together. One partner in a major venture-capital firm explained why he didn't like one entrepreneur's plan. 'This has been laid out immaculately with bookbinding and typeset pages and as a consequence it doesn't come across as a custom document assembled for targeted investors. In other words, our needs have either been ignored or treated as being identical to any other source of money. Neither of these views is particularly appealing.'

Consensus seems to favour a plastic-spiral binding, holding together a pair of single-colour cover sheets. This will look pleasant and be strong enough to survive being handled by a number of people.

Wide margins and 1.5 line spacing are also in favour, making it easier to read the plan and make notes while reading.

- Potential lenders are looking for evidence that the entrepreneur takes care over his or her own property and is therefore also likely to handle the investor's funds carefully. Spelling mistakes, poor grammar, typing errors and a generally untidy layout are all minus points in that respect.
- No business plan should exceed 40 pages, and most should be no longer than 20. It may be necessary to produce a separate volume of appendices, but the whole of the business arguments and funding requirements must be kept to a minimum.

Although the first draft of a business plan may be much longer than the recommended length, editing must produce a final version that fits within our target of 20–40 pages.

George Bernard Shaw is reputed to have added this postscript to a long letter sent to a friend in England: 'If I'd had more time I would have sent you a postcard.'

Layout and content

There is resistance among financial institutions to hard-and-fast rules on the layout and content of a business plan. This is understandable as every business and investor is different, and the standard approach taken by lawyers to wills and contracts is seen as out of place in the world of enterprise.

That being said, experience shows that certain layouts and contents have gone down better than others. These are some guidelines to producing an attractive business plan, from the investor's point of view. Not every subheading will be relevant to every type of business, but the general format should be followed, with emphasis laid as appropriate.

The cover and title page

Surprising though it may seem, a large number of business plans are submitted without any essential factual information as to how to contact the entrepreneur. They may well have written a covering letter giving some of this detail, but it is the business plan itself that gets passed around in financiers' offices.

The cover should contain the name of the company seeking funds, its address and phone number and the date on which the plan was issued. This date should confirm that this plan is the company's latest view on its position and financing needs.

The title page, immediately behind the front cover, should once again show the name and address of the company, and it should also give the chief executive's name, address and phone number. He or she is likely to be the first point of contact and anyone reading the business plan may want to talk over some aspects of the proposal before arranging a meeting.

In an upper corner, show the words 'copy number –'. This is important for at least two reasons. First, you are sending out extremely confidential information concerning your future plans, so only a limited number of copies should be in circulation and you should have a record of who has a copy.

Second, the prospective financier won't want to think he or she is receiving a proposal that has been hawked around the city, so a double figure number here is likely to switch him or her off. Remember your business plan should be targeted as specific sources of finance. It's highly likely, therefore, that you will need to assemble slightly different business plans, highlighting areas of concern to lenders as opposed to investors, for example. Each modification needs a new numbering sequence.

The executive summary

No longer than two pages, this follows immediately behind the title page. Over a third of business plans received by financiers still don't have an executive summary. A further third have one that is inadequate, inaccurate, or incomplete.

This is the most important single part of the business plan and will probably do more than anything else you do to influence whether or not the plan is reviewed in its entirety. It can also make the reader favourably disposed towards a venture at the outset, which is no bad thing.

These two pages must explain clearly and concisely:

1. The current state of the company in respect of product/service readiness for market; trading position and past successes if already running; and key staff on board.
2. The products or services to be sold and to whom they will be sold, including detail on competitive advantage.
3. The reasons why customers need this product or service, together with some indication of market size and growth.
4. The company's aims and objectives both in the immediate future and two to five years ahead, and an indication of the strategies to be employed in getting there.
5. The financial forecasts, sales, profits, cash flow, etc.
6. How much money is needed.
7. How and when the investor or lender will benefit from providing the funds.

This may seem a near impossible task, but it can and should be done. The three minutes or so needed to read the executive summary could be the most important in the company's entire life – either turning on, or off, a potential investor.

Obviously, the executive summary can only be written after the business plan itself has been completed.

The table of contents

After the executive summary follows a table of contents. This is the map that will guide the new readers through your business proposal and on to the 'inevitable' conclusion that they should put up the funds. If a map is obscure, muddled or even missing, the chances are you will end up with lost or even irritated readers unable to find their way around your proposal.

Each of the main sections of the business plan should be listed and the pages within that section indicated. There are two valid schools of thought on page numbering. One favours a straightforward sequential numbering of each page 1, 2, 3… 19, 20, and so on. This seems to me to be perfectly adequate for short, simple plans dealing with uncomplicated issues and seeking modest levels of finance.

More ambitious proposals may call for section numbering. For example, the section headed 'The Business and its Management' might be Section 1 in some business plans. In that case the pages would be identified from 1.1 to 1.8 in the table of contents, so identifying each page within that section as belonging to that specific section. Tables and figures should also bear page numbers that relate to the section in which they are found.

Individual paragraph numbering, much in favour with government and civil service departments, is considered something of an overkill in a business plan and is to be discouraged, except perhaps if you are looking for a large amount of government grant.

The table of contents on page 181 shows both the layout and content that in our experience is most in favour with financial institutions.

For the most part the remaining headings in this table of contents are reasonably self-explanatory. The financial elements of the business plan are comprehensively covered elsewhere in this book, but two areas deserve a special mention at this stage: the deal on offer and how much your business is worth.

The deal on offer

For borrowed money the 'deal on offer' will revolve around negotiating interest rates, repayment periods and perhaps collateral and security arrangements – all relatively simple concepts covering 'easy to measure' areas of business.

For equity capital, involving the sale of a share of your business, the problems are more complex and you need to consider the following issues before preparing a deal.

How much is your business worth?

The formula used by venture-capital providers to value a business is conceptually simple, but the factors used in the equation itself are somewhat subjective. The following example shows how the worth of a business can be calculated.

Example
Cranfield Engineering Ltd
Cranfield Engineering Ltd (CEL) is a new start-up business which needs a £200,000 equity injection to achieve its business plan objectives. A brief summary of its financial projections is shown in Table 10.1.

Table 10.1 Cranfield Engineering Ltd financial projections

	Turnover	Profit after tax
Year 1	£200,000	(£25,000)
Year 2	£500,000	£100,000
Year 3	£750,000	£200,000

Assuming that a P/E ratio (ie the ratio of a share's price to its earning) of 10 is used as the accepted multiplier of earnings in the industry,* then using the formula:

$$\text{Present value (PV)} = \frac{\text{Future valuation (FV)}}{(1 + i)^n}$$

where FV = Maintainable profits $\times$ Applicable P/E ratio

and

i = Required rate of return (to investor)
n = Number of years until date of forecast earnings used to calculate valuation

Assuming that the figures provided by CEL are accepted at face value (which is unlikely) and that maintainable profits are achieved in year 2, and that our investor is seeking a 60 per cent return (because of the high risk involved), then the valuation of the company would be as follows:

$$PV = \frac{£(100,000 \times 10)}{(1 + 0.60)^2} = \frac{£1,000,000}{2.56} = £390,625$$

*For private companies the P/E ratio varies by business sector; for example bio-tech companies can be on multiples of 50 or 60, while retailers may be on 12. The stage in the economic cycle can make a different. In 2000 average exit P/Es for private companies were around 12. By 1993 it was around 5.

If the company is valued at £390,625 and CEL requires £200,000, then the percentage of the equity that the investor will acquire will be:

$$\frac{200,000}{390,625} \times 100 = 51.2\%$$

Obviously, while the above is mathematically correct, there would be much negotiation about the acceptability of the factors being used and perhaps on which years' profits represent 'maintainable profits'; in the above example, if year 3 had been used, then the investor's share of the equity would have fallen to 41 per cent.

How can you retain control?

While the equation above will show how much equity should be sold to realise a given sum of money, the business proprietor is also concerned with retaining control of the venture. It's important to realise that it is possible to retain 51 per cent of the shares. This can be done by including a restriction on voting rights in your negotiations with any potential investor. A well-known example of this A/B share type structure is the Savoy Hotel Group, in which Trusthouse Forte had the majority of the shares, some 70 per cent, but only a minority of the voting shares.

It is also important to remember that 'control' is more to do with ability, skill and entrepreneurial talent than about having the majority of shares. After all, Anita Roddick, founder of the Body Shop and Richard Branson of Virgin are minority shareholders in their own companies, but no one doubts who is in control of their respective businesses.

Exit routes for outside investors

Although your time horizons may be long term and your rewards partially satisfied by non-financial things – running your own business, freedom, etc – potential investors are not similarly disposed. They have their own set investment criteria, outlined above, and prior to investment they must have identified an exit route within an acceptable time-scale. The most likely exit routes are:

Disposal to a trade buyer

Either you or your investor finds a larger company in a similar or complementary business and sells out to them. This is probably the number one exit method in terms of frequency, although it is not without its risks.

Share repurchase by entrepreneur(s)

The outside investor is bought out by the management team, usually on preferential terms, with assisted funding. This is the least popular route, commonly regarded as the option for 'also rans' which failed to match expectations.

Public share quotation

On the stock markets. While this is the less likely route, it must be the aspiration of both entrepreneur and outside investor alike. Anita Roddick of the Body Shop and Tom Farmer of Kwik-Fit are just two of the many millionaire entrepreneurs who have taken their business to the stock market.

Table 10.2   Sample table of contents

Section	Page or Sequential Pages	
Executive Summary	i, ii	i, ii
1. The Business and Its Management	1.1	1, etc
History and Position to Date	1.2	
Current or New Mission	1.3	
Objectives, Near Term	1.4	
Objectives, Long Term	1.5	
The Management Team	1.6	
Legal Structure	1.7	
Professional Advisers	1.8	
2. The Products or Services		
Descriptions	2.1	
Readiness for Market	2.2	
Applications	2.3	

Appendices could include:

- management team biographies;
- names and details of professional advisers;
- technical data and drawings;
- details of patents, copyright, designs;
- audited accounts;

- consultants' reports, or other published data on products, markets, etc;
- orders on hand and enquiry status;
- detailed market-research methods and findings;
- organisation charts.

NB. Additional separate entries for tables and figures should be provided using the same page numbering method, eg: Competitor Data, Table 1.1, page 3.7, etc.

Writing and editing

The first draft of your business plan should be written by yourself and your management team. Each person involved should write up the part of the plan for which he or she is directly responsible, eg the production director writes up 'manufacturing' and the sales director 'selling'. Each section should then be circulated for comments and criticisms. This is usually the moment when tempers flare, but it is also the point where the managing director can exercise his or her talents for smoothing ruffled feathers and welding a group of people, pulling in different directions, into a coherent team.

Don't worry too much that each section has been written in a different style; this and other matters of presentation can be dealt with later.

Once the first draft of the business plan has been agreed, it should be submitted to the firm's professional advisers. Lawyers and accountants have considerable experience in dealing with investors, bankers and the Stock Exchange, so they will know how best to present the facts you have assembled. They will also advise on the appropriate language to be used when making statements; for example, a statement that investors will receive a return of at least 100 per cent annually on their investment could result in an unwelcome visit from the Fraud Squad if forecasts are not subsequently achieved.

This would also be a good time to talk the proposal over with a 'friendly' bankers or venture-capital provider. He or she can give an insider's view as to what needs beefing up or playing down.

After the first draft of the business plan has been reviewed by the management team and their professional advisers comes the task of moulding it into a readable document that prospective investors will find attractive. This will call for a professional examination of such matters as: syntax, grammar, spelling, consistency, clarity, elimination of jargon and repetition, and the business plan's overall organisation. There is absolutely no doubt that a well-written business plan is better received than one that is poorly written, so take advice. Freelance business journalists, editors of trade magazines, regional journalists, English teachers, librarians and professional freelance editors are all people accustomed to simplifying and organising language and expressing ideas in a way that will keep their audience's interest.

Before any business plan is sent out to any prospective investor or lender it should be carefully proofread – misspellings and typing mistakes carry a strong negative message to financiers.

Who to send it to

Now you are ready to send out your business plan to a few carefully selected financial institutions who you know are interested in proposals such as yours. The British Venture Capital Association (address on page 223) has over 200 member-organisations that are involved in the provision of venture capital. A list of these members, together with useful details such as members' investment and industry preferences, is published annually as the *BVCA Directory*. The BVCA also publishes *A Directory of Business Introduction Services*, linking entrepreneurs to business angels within the UK.

This will involve some research into the particular interests, foibles and idiosyncrasies of the institutions themselves. If you are only interested in raising debt capital, the field is narrowed to the clearing banks, for the main part. If you are looking for someone to share the risk with you, you must review the much wider field of venture capital. Here some institutions will only look at proposals over a certain capital sum, such as £250,000, or will only invest in certain technologies.

It would be as well to carry out this research before the final editing of your business plan, as you should incorporate something of this knowledge in the way your business plan is presented. You may well find that slightly different versions of Section 8.5, 'The Deal on Offer', have to be made up for each different source of finance to which you send your business plan.

Finally, how long will it all take? This also depends on whether you are raising debt or equity, the institution you approach and the complexity of the deal on offer. A secured bank loan, for example, can take from a few days to a few weeks to arrange.

Investment from a venture-capital house will rarely take less than three months to arrange, more usually take six, and could even take up to nine. Though the deal itself may be struck early on, the lawyers will pore over the detail for weeks. Every exchange of letters can add a fortnight to the wait. So timing is another factor to consider when deciding who to send your plan to and what sort of finance to raise – and the timing will have to be allowed for in your projections.

The oral presentation

If getting someone interested in your business plan is half the battle in raising funds, the other half is the oral presentation. Any organisation financing a venture will insist on seeing the team involved presenting and defending their plans – in person. They know that they are backing people every bit as much as the idea, and you need to have that fact in mind before you make the presentation.

Financiers will be looking at the following factors when an entrepreneur and his team appear before them:

- How well prepared is the management team for the presentation? No visuals, muddled cues and misunderstandings between team members will all be taken as adverse signs. The managing director should introduce the team and orchestrate the individual contributions.
- How clearly and coherently does the team explain the business concept, the products, markets, their organisation and its appropriateness for this venture?
- Does the team come across as market orientated, with realistic aims, a proper regard for profits and cash flow, and a clear understanding of competitive market forces?
- How well does the team sell itself and defend its proposals?
- Do the team members appear receptive to constructive criticism and advice?
- Do members of the team exhibit integrity, appear appropriately

dressed –and if the financiers are coming to your office, do they seem workmanlike and appropriate too?

- Is it a good product? Demonstrate the product if at all possible, or offer to take the financiers to see it in operation elsewhere. One entrepreneur arranged to have his product, a computer-controlled camera system for monitoring product quality in engineering processes, on free loan to Ford for the three months he was looking for money. This not only helped financiers to understand the application of a complex product, but the benefit of seeing it at work in a prestigious major company was incalculable.

- What empathy is there between the financiers and the entrepreneurs? You may not be able to change your personalities but you could take a few tips on public speaking. Eye contact, tone of speech, enthusiasm and body language all play their part in making the interview go well, so read up on this and rehearse the presentation before an audience.

Entrepreneurs can assume that financiers will have already begun their process of 'due diligence', the procedure by which all proposals are vetted, by the time they get to making a presentation. They will have done some preliminary research to check out the potential market, competition, customers and the claims made for the product or service. They may even have checked out the records of former employers, county court judgements and the like to satisfy themselves as to the integrity and financial probity of the entrepreneur and his or her team. It should also be noted that financiers, venture capitalists in particular, are a closely knit community and often share information on ventures they are considering backing. They often syndicate investments, spreading a share of the risk and reward with other like-minded institutions. So if unfavourable information falls into one investor's hands it can spread quickly to a much wider audience. Honesty is always the best policy and many financiers are more interested in hearing what you learned from earlier business failures that will make this one a winner than in allocating blame for the past.

11 *Bookkeeping and flash reports*

It is hard to believe that any businessperson could hope to survive without knowing how much cash he or she has, and what the profit or loss on sales is. These facts are needed on at least a monthly, weekly, or occasionally even a daily basis to survive, let alone grow.

And yet all too often a new business's first set of accounts are also its last, with the firm's accountant, bank manager or creditors signalling bankruptcy. While bad luck plays a part in some failures, a lack of reliable financial information plays a part in most. The chapters on financial controls show the wealth of vital facts that can be put at the decision makers' finger-tips. That is, if only they could be bothered to assemble the basic information as it comes in.

But it is not only the owner who needs these financial facts. Bankers, shareholders, the Inland Revenue and the Customs and Excise (VAT) will be unsympathetic audiences to the businessman without well-documented facts to back him up. The Inland Revenue, for example, will present a new business with a tax demand. The onus then lies with the businessperson to use his or her records, and either to agree or dispute the sum that the Inland Revenue claims. A bank manager, faced with a request for an increased overdraft facility to help a small business grow, needs financial facts to work with. Without them he or she will generally have to say no, as a bank manager is responsible for other people's money.

Why you need proper records

All the information needed to manage a business well is close at hand. The bills to be paid, invoices raised, petty-cash slips and bank statements alone are enough to give a true picture of performance. All that needs to be done is for that information to be recorded and organised so that the financial picture becomes clear. The way financial information is recorded is known as 'bookkeeping'.

But it is not only the owner of a company who needs these financial facts. As we have noted, bankers, shareholders and tax inspectors will be unsympathetic to anyone without well-documented facts to back them up. If, for example, a tax authority presents a business with a tax demand, the onus then lies with the business to consult its records, then dispute or provide the sum demanded using these as reference. If you are unable to adequately explain a bank deposit, the tax authority may treat it as taxable income. A bank manager faced with a request from a small business for an increased overdraft facility to help it grow needs financial facts to work with. Without them, the manager will generally have to say no, as he or she has been given the responsibility to look after the money by its owners.

Keeping even the simplest of records – perhaps as little as writing down the source of the deposit on the slip or in your chequebook – and recording the event in a book or ledger will make your relations with tax inspectors and bankers go much more smoothly.

If you just pile your bills, receipts and cheque stubs into an old shoebox and take it to an accountant at the end of the year (or when you run out of cash), it will cost a lot more to get your accounts done than if you had kept good records in the first place. In addition, you will have a stressful time, as you will not be sure how well or badly your business is doing.

Starting simple

If you are keeping your books by hand and don't have a lot of transactions, the 'single-entry' method is the easiest and most acceptable way to go. Single-entry means you write down each transaction in your records once – preferably on a ledger sheet. You record the flow of income and expenses through your business by making a running total of money taken in ('gross receipts') and money paid out ('payments', or as they are sometimes called, 'disbursements'). Receipts and payments should be kept and summarised daily, weekly or monthly in accordance with the requirements of the business. At the end of the year, the 12 monthly summaries are totalled up – you are ready for tax time.

An example of a 'cash book', as this simple record system is known, is shown in Table 11.1.

In the left-hand four columns of Table 11.1, the month's expenses are entered as they occur, together with some basic details and the amount. At the head of the fourth column is the amount of cash brought forward from the preceding month.

On the right, expenses are listed in the same way. The total receipts for the month are £1,480.15 and expenses £672.01. The difference is the amount of cash currently in the business. As more cash has been brought in than has been spent, the figure is higher than the amount brought forward at the beginning of the month. This figure of £808.14 is the amount we 'bring down' to be 'brought forward' to the next month. The total of the month's payments and the amount 'brought down' is equal to the sum of all the receipts in the left-hand columns.

If there is a reasonably large number of transactions it would be sensible to extend this simple cash book to include a basic analysis of the figures.

An example of the payments side of an analysed cash book is shown in Table 11.2 (the receipts side is similar but with different categories). You can see at a glance the receipts and payments both in total and by main category. This breakdown lets you see, amongst other things, how much is being spent on each major area of your business and who your most important customers are. The payments are the same as in Table 11.1, but now we can see how much has been spent on stock, vehicles and telephone expenses. The sums total both down the

Table 11.1 A simple cash book system

Receipts				Payments			
Date	Name	Details	Amount £	Date	Name	Details	Amount £
1 June	Balance	Brought forward	450.55	4 June	Gibbs	Stock purchase	310
4 June	Anderson	Sales	175	8 June	Gibbs	Stock purchase	130
6 June	Brown	Sales	45	12 June	ABC Telecoms	Telephone charges	55.23
14 June	Smith & Co	Refund on returned stock	137.34	18 June	Colt Rentals	Vehicle hire	87.26
17 June	Jenkins	Sales	190.25	22 June	VW Mobiles	Mobile phone	53.24
20 June	Hollis	Sales	425.12	27 June	Gibbs	Stock purchase	36.28
23 June	Jenkins	Sales	56.89				
							672.01
				30 June	Balance	Carried down	808.14
			1,480.15				1,480.15
1 July	Balance	Brought down	808.14				

amount columns and across the analysis section, to arrive at the same amount. £672.01. This provides useful management information, as well as being essential for your tax return.

If you are taking or giving credit, you will need to keep more information than just the cash book, even if it is analysed.

Table 11.2   Example of an analysed cash book

Payments				Analysis			
Date	Name	Details	Amount £	Stocks	Vehicles	Telephone	Other
4 June	Gibbs	Stock purchase	310	310			
8 June	Gibbs	Stock purchase	130	130			
12 June	ABC Telecoms	Telephone charges	55.23			55.23	
18 June	Colt Rentals	Vehicle hire	87.26		87.26		
22 June	VW Mobiles	Mobile phone	53.24			53.24	
27 June	Gibbs	Stock purchase	36.28	36.28			
Totals			672.01	476.28	87.26	108.47	

You will need copies of paid and unpaid sales invoices and records of purchases, as well as your bank statements. The bank statements should be 'reconciled' to your cash book to tie everything together. For example, the bank statement for the example given in Table 11.1 should show £808.14 in the account at the end of June. Figure 11.1 outlines how this works.

Building a system

If you operate a partnership, trade as a company or plan to get big, you will need a double-entry bookkeeping system. This will call for a series of day books, ledgers, a journal, a petty-cash book and a wages book, as well as a number of files for copies of invoices and receipts.

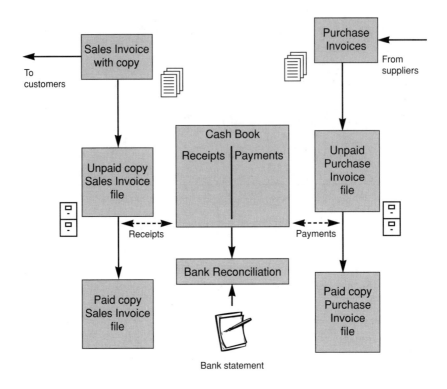

Figure 11.1 A simple system of business records

This bookkeeping system requires two entries for each transaction, which provide built-in checks and balances to ensure accuracy. Each transaction requires an entry as a debit and as a credit. This may sound a little complicated, but you only need to understand the general idea.

A double-entry system is more complicated and time consuming if done by hand, as everything is recorded twice. If done manually, the method requires a formal set of books – journals and ledgers. All transactions are first entered into a journal and are then 'posted' (written) on a ledger sheet – the same amount is written down in two different places. Typical ledger accounts are: titled income, expenses, assets and liabilities (debts).

To give an example, in a double-entry system, a payment of rent might result in two separate journal entries – a debit for an expense of, say, £250 and a corresponding credit of £250: a double entry. The debits in a double entry must always equal the credits. If they don't, you know there is an error somewhere. So, double entry allows you to balance your books, which you can't do with the single-entry method.

Table 11.3 An example of a double-entry ledger

General Journal of Andrew's Bookshop

Date	Description of entry	Debit	Credit
10th July	Rent expense	£250	
	Cash		£250

Below is a list of the records that need to be kept under the double-entry system.

Day books

Day books, sometimes called 'journals' or 'books of original entry', are where every transaction is initially recorded in date order. Each day book is used to cater for one particular kind of transaction, so if there are enough transactions of a particular kind, you should open a day book for them. For example, there are always enough cash transactions to warrant a cash day book. If a firm sells on credit, then there will be a sales day book. Cash day books are described below.

Cash books

Many small businesses trade in notes, coins and cheques. For book-keeping purposes, they are all classed as cash, although a separate record should initially be kept of each.

The petty-cash book is used to record transactions in notes and coins. Money in is recorded on the left-hand page and money out is on the right. The money-out column may include items such as stamps or office coffee. Always keep receipts, as one day you may have to verify the records. Once a week (or daily if the sums involved justify it), total the money in and money out to get a cash balance. Check that it agrees with actual cash in the till or cash box.

The cash book records all receipts and payments made by cheque. Once again, money in is on the left-hand page and money out is on the right. Every week, add up both pages to arrive at a cash bank balance. This should be checked against your bank statement at least once a month to ensure that the basic information you are working with is correct.

Sales ledgers and purchase ledgers

If your business gives credit to customers or takes credit from suppliers, you will need a sales ledger and a purchase ledger. Each ledger should ideally have a separate page for every business that you deal with.

On the right-hand side of the purchase ledger are listed the date, description, amount, and cost of each item bought on credit. On the left-hand side, a record is kept of all payments made to the supplier along with the items for which the payments were made. Each month, by deducting the left-hand total from the right, you can see how much each supplier is owed. Suppliers ought to send you a statement and you can use this to check your own version of the accounts.

The sales ledger deals with customers in much the same way. One important difference is that credit sales are shown on the left-hand side of the ledger and customers' payments appear on the right. This is simply an accounting convention to deal with credits and debits. It is very useful to keep notes of customers' (and suppliers') addresses, telephone numbers and contact names with each entry in the ledgers. This will ensure you have all the relevant information when chasing up payments or dealing with queries.

Capital or asset registers

Limited companies have to keep a capital register. This records the capital items owned by a company, such as land, buildings, equipment and vehicles, and shows their cost at date of purchase. The capital register also records the disposal of any of these items and the cumulative depreciation.

Nominal (or 'private') ledgers

These are usually kept by your accountant or bookkeeper. A nominal ledger brings together all the information from the 'primary ledgers' (the basic records). Expenses from the cash books and the purchase ledger are 'posted' to the left-hand side of the nominal ledger. Income from sales (and any other income) are posted to the right. Normally, each type of expense or income has a separate page – this makes subsequent analysis an easier task.

The trial balance

Every month, each page in the nominal ledger is totalled, and used to prepare a trial balance. In other words, the sum of all the left-hand totals should end up equalling the sum of all the right-hand totals. This is the basis of double-entry bookkeeping, and is what gives you confidence that the figures are correctly recorded.

Using a computer

With the cost of a basic computerised accounting system starting at around £50, and a reasonable package costing between £200 and £500, it makes good sense to plan to use such a system from the outset. Some advantages of using a computerised system are:

- **No more arithmetic errors.** As long as the information is entered correctly, it will be added up correctly. With a computer, the £250 rent expenditure in the example above is input as an expense (a debit), and then the computer automatically posts it to the rent account as a credit. In effect, the computer eliminates the extra step of the need to master the difference between debit and credit.
- **Routine tasks take minutes rather than days.** Chores such as filling in the tax returns, VAT and so on become much quicker. A computerised system can enable you to see immediately whether your returns are accurate and fully reconciled. Also, you can see at a glance the customers who are regularly taking too long to pay and reminder statements can be automatically prepared.

- **You can match stock levels to demand.** If your business is concerned with stockholding, a computerised system can help you keep track of these. It can even provide profit-margin information quickly by product, so you can see which products are worth promoting and which are less attractive.
- **Your year-end accounts preparation and audit will be greatly streamlined.** This will save time and money, and allow you to monitor profits and cash flow easily.

A halfway house to having computerised accounts is to use a spreadsheet. This is useful if your business has relatively few transactions each month – say, no more than 20 or 30 items to record. Using a spreadsheet won't give you the advantages of a double-entry accounting system, but with this number of records, the chances are you won't need them. Using a spreadsheet will reduce the chances of arithmetic errors, save time spent adding and subtracting columns and make the calculations in an analysed cash book easier to do. If you already have a spreadsheet, the only additional cost is the time spent working out the sums to use and preparing the spreadsheet.

Two suppliers with a good range of accounting products are:

The Sage Group Plc
Sage House
Benton Park Road
Newcastle upon Tyne NE7 7LZ

Tel: 0191 255 3000
Fax: 0191 255 0308
Web site: www.sage.com

QuickBooks
Intuit Service Centre
Freepost SCE 127
Swindon, Wilts SN5 8ZZ

Tel: 0800 585058
Fax: 0845 6011571
Web site: www.intuit.co.uk

Monthly flash reports

Until accruals have been dealt with, a physical stocktake has been carried out and a business's books have been audited or examined, final accounts cannot be produced. However, the information from the ledgers *can* be used to produce a flash report each month to show how the business appears to be performing.

A profit-and-loss account can be prepared; the cash-book balances can show the cash in hand; the purchase and sales ledgers can show how much the business owes and is owed. In addition, many of the control ratios on profitability and liquidity can be prepared. All this can be compared with your plan or budget to see if the company's performance is on target.

This information will complement an entrepreneur's natural flair with some hard facts. It will also give him or her time to overcome problems before they become unmanageable.

12 *Improving performance*

Areas of poor or declining financial performance identified whilst monitoring performance against budget may be improved by taking one or more of a number of actions. The most fruitful places to look for better results are the prices, costs and capital employed in the day-to-day running of the business.

Pricing for profit

Small firms are often guilty of getting their prices wrong at first. The misconception that new and small firms can undercut established competitors is usually based on ignorance of either the true costs of a product or service, or of the true value of overheads.

The overhead argument usually runs like this: 'The competition is big, has plush offices, and lots of overpaid marketing executives spending the company's money on expense-account lunches, and I don't have any of these. Ergo, I *must* be able to undercut them.' The errors within this type of argument are, first, that the plush office, far from being an unnecessary overhead, is actually a fast-appreciating asset, perhaps even generating more profit than the company's main products (shops, restaurants, and hotels typically fit into this category). The plush office can also contribute to creating an image for the product or service in such a way that enhances its price – Harley Street consultants, for example, fit into this category. Second, the marketing executives may be paid more than you pay and may have expense accounts, but if they do not deliver a constant stream of new products and new strategies to justify the money spent, they will be replaced with people who can.

Clearly, you have to take account of what your competitors charge, but remember: price is the easiest element of the marketing mix for an established company to vary. The competition could copy your lower prices, forcing you into a price war and possible bankruptcy, far more easily than you could capture their customers with lower prices.

Whilst most small firms – 80 per cent according to some reports – set their price with reference to costs either using a cost-plus formula (for example, the cost of materials plus 50 per cent) or a cost-multiplier formula (for example, three times materials costs), all *customers* buy with reference to *value*. That can leave a lot of scope for managing your prices up.

Price is the element of the marketing mix that is likely to have the greatest impact on the profitability of small businesses. It is often more profitable for a new company to sell fewer items at a higher price whilst getting its organisation and product offerings sorted out; the key is to concentrate on obtaining good margins, often with a range of prices and quality.

Using the data from the example of the High Note profit-and-loss account in Chapter 5 (page 68), we can see what might have happened had they raised their prices rather than increased their sales volume from £100,000 to £130,000. It is not an unreasonable assumption, for the purposes of this illustration, to suggest that all this growth came from selling more to more customers. Had they raised their prices by 5 per cent and lost no customers, then they would have made £5,000 more gross profit. As the expenses have all been met, we can assume that all of this will drop to the bottom line.

If, as a consequence of putting up their prices, they had lost 5 per cent of their customers, the sum would look like this: sales would go down to £95,000 in volume terms, but the gross margin on those sales would rise from 50 per cent to 55 per cent, as more is being charged. That would produce a gross profit of £52,250 (£95,000 × 55 per cent). Expenses would remain at £33,000, leaving an operating profit of £19,250. That is £2,500 higher than the £17,000 we would have made on the higher volume of sales made at the original lower price.

Working through the rest of the figures in the same way, we can see that unless it is considered that more than 10 per cent of business would be lost by putting prices up by 5 per cent, there shouldn't be a problem. Putting prices up by 15 per cent will deliver higher profits, even if more than15 per cent of the business is lost. In fact, High Note could afford to lose over 20 per cent of its business and still be better off (see Table 12.1).

Table 12.1   The effect of raising prices

Change in profits £000s (+/–%) at varying volume losses

Change in price	0%	–5%	–10%	–15%
+5%	5	2.25	–0.5	–3.25
+10%	10	7	4	1
+15%	15	11.75	8.5	5.25

The above sums depend upon your level of gross profit. In High Notes's case, this was 50 per cent. The lower your gross profit, the less business you can afford to lose for any given price rise. But there are some benefits to this method that have not been shown. Putting the pressure on price rather than volume means carrying less stock, having fewer bills to chase, using less capital and wearing out equipment less quickly.

This is not to imply that putting up prices is an easy task. But it may not be much harder than finding new customers, and is nearly always more profitable.

Reducing costs

Costs are associated with activity. But, as activity is often allocated wrongly, it follows that the opportunity for cost reduction is almost always greater than you think.

This is demonstrated by the 80/20 rule – the Pareto principle. You can test this principle by looking at your own business. A close examination of your client list will show that 20 per cent of them account for the vast majority of your business and perhaps all of your profit. Yet you spend as much time servicing unprofitable customers as you do profitable ones.

What makes cost reduction so powerful is the disproportionate effect on profits that even a small reduction in costs can have. Look at Table 12.2; you can see that, for a business making a 5 per cent net profit, reducing costs by just 2 per cent will raise profits by 40 per cent from £50,000 to £70,000. The company may well have needed to find 10 per cent or even 20 per cent more customers to have the same effect on the only place that matters: the bottom line.

Table 12.2 Cost savings matter

	Before		After 2% cost saving		Extra performance	
	£000s	%	£000s	%	£000s	%
Sales	1,000	100	1,000	100	–	–
Costs	950	95	930	93	–20	–2
Profit	50	5	70	7	+20	+40

Squeezing working capital

Once you have bought your shop, set up your factory or bought your delivery vehicle, they are 'sunk' costs. You may want more, but you are limited by the amount of capital. However, you do have discretion over your working capital; the more you squeeze it, the less money you have tied up in the business for a given level of activity. That, in turn, means lower borrowing costs.

The evidence points to small firms being inefficient users of working capital. The smaller they are, the less efficient they tend to be (see Figure 12.1).

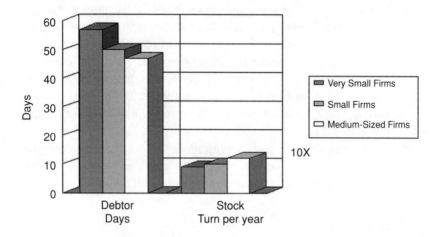

Figure 12.1   Very small firms can have poor control of working capital

Here are some things you can do to make better use of your working capital:

- Find out when your biggest customers have their monthly cheque run and make sure your bills reach them in time.
- Send out statements promptly to chase up late payers and always follow up with a phone call.
- Always take trade references when giving credit and look at the client's accounts to see how sound they are.
- Have accurate stock records and monitor slow-moving stock.
- Have an accurate sales-forecasting system (a sound budgeting process will do) so you can match stock and work according to likely demand.
- Take credit from your suppliers up to the maximum time allowed. Try and negotiate extended terms with major suppliers once you have a good track record. Many will say no, but some may not. The advent of a price rise is a good moment to begin negotiating.

● Make any cash you have work harder. Use overnight money markets via an Internet bank to get interest on cash rather than having it sitting in the banking system earning you nothing.
● Work out whether it makes sense to pay bills quickly to take advantage of early-settlement discounts. Sometimes – usually by accident – suppliers offer what amounts to high rates of interest for settling up promptly. If you are offered 2½ per cent to pay up now rather than in two months time, that is equivalent to an annual rate of interest of 15 per cent (12/2 × 2½ per cent). If your bank is charging you 8 per cent, then you will make a good extra profit by taking up this offer.
● Bank cheques and cash promptly. It's not only safer, but the sooner you get money into the banking system, the sooner you are either saving interest cost or earning interest income.

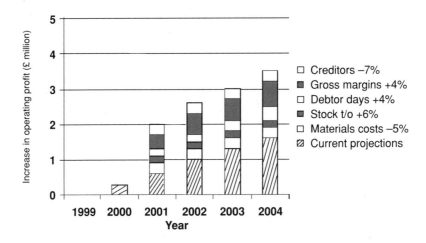

Figure 12.2 Releasing hidden profitability

The profit-improvement programme

Once you have completed your review of past performance and identified the areas for improvement, you need to prepare an action plan to show exactly how all this hidden profit is to be released.

Set improvement targets for each area, as shown in the Figure 12.2. The tasks identified as needed to achieve these results should be incorporated into your next budget review. Where an opportunity to improve is substantial and the work involved is minimal, 'seize the hour' and start improving profits straight away.

Answers to questions

Chapter 1

1. If you net worth is more than you thought, buy a bottle of champagne and celebrate. (If not, do same and drown your sorrows.)
2. Balance sheet at Sunday 24 April

Net assets employed	£	£	£
Fixed assets			
Factory premises		18,000	
Equipment and machinery		7,600	25,600
Current assets			
Stock	1,400		
Debtors	1,400		
Cash	800	3,600	
Less Current liabilities			
Creditors	(1,800)		
Tax due	(700)	(2,500)	
Net current assets			1,100
			26,700
Financed by			
Owner's capital introduced	18,700		
Less drawings	(4,000)		14,700
Long-term loan			12,000
			26,700

Chapter 2

		1 £	2 £	3 £	4 £	5 £
1.	Fixed assets	–	15,000	18,000	18,000	18,000
	Working capital					
	Current assets					
	Stock	1,550	1,550	1,550	4,550	2,750
	Debtors	–	–	–	–	2,700
	Cash	13,700	12,200	12,200	12,200	12,200
		15,250	13,750	13,750	16,750	17,650
	Less Current liabilities					
	Overdraft	5,000	5,000	5,000	5,000	5,000
	Creditors	–	–	3,000	6,000	6,000
		5,000	5,000	8,000	11,000	11,000
	Net current assets	10,250	8,750	5,750	5,750	6,650
	Total assets	10,250	23,750	23,750	23,750	24,650
	Financed by					
	Share capital	10,000	10,000	10,000	10,000	10,000
	Reserves	250	250	250	250	1,150
		10,250	10,250	10,250	10,250	11,150
	Mortgage	–	13,500	13,500	13,500	13,500
		10,250	23,750	23,750	23,750	24,650

		£
2.	Sales	174,000
	Cost of sales	
	Opening stock	110,000
	Purchases	90,000
		200,000
	Less Closing stock	73,700
	Cost of goods sold	126,300

Gross profit	47,700

Operating expenses	
Selling	7,000
Administration	21,000
Advertising	2,100
Miscellaneous	1,900
	32,000

Operating profit	15,700
Rent received	400
	16,100

Loan interest paid	3,000
	13,100

Provision for Income Tax	3,275
Net profit after tax	9,825

Chapter 3

1. **High Note – balance sheet at end September**

Fixed assets	£	£
Fixtures and fittings		12,500
Working capital		
Current assets		
Stock	9,108	
Debtors	12,000	
Cash	–	
	21,108	
Less Current liabilities		
Overdraft needed	4,908	
Creditors	–	
	4,908	
Net current assets		16,200

Total capital employed		28,700

Financed by

Owner's capital	10,000
Profit retained	8,700
Long-term loan	10,000
	28,700

2.

Cash receipts in	April £	May £	June £	July £	Aug £	Sept £
Sales	5,000	6,000	6,000	8,000	13,000	16,000
Owner's capital	10,000					
Loan capital	10,000					
Total cash in	25,000	6,000	6,000	8,000	13,000	16,000
Cash payments out						
Purchases	5,500	2,950	4,220	7,416	9,332	9,690
Rent, rates, etc	2,300	2,300	2,300	2,300	2,300	2,300
Wages	1,000	1,000	1,000	1,000	1,000	1,000
Advertising	250	250	250	250	250	250
Fixtures and fittings	10,500	–	–	–	–	–
Total cash out	19,550	6,500	7,770	10,966	12,882	13,240
Cash balances						
Monthly cash balance	5,450	(500)	(1,770)	(2,996)	118	2,760
Balance brought forward	–	5,450	4,950	3,180	184	302
Balance to carry forward or net cash flow	5,450	4,950	3,180	184	302	3,062

Comment. Now you can see how significant quite minor changes in assumptions can be.

3. **Part 1: Profit-and-loss account unchanged.**
   Part 2: Balance sheet

	£	£
Fixed assets		
Fixtures and fittings		10,500
Working capital		
Current assets		
Stock	9,108	
Debtors	6,000	
Cash	3,092	
	18,200	
Less Current liabilities	–	
Creditors		
Net current assets		18,200
Total capital employed		28,700
Financed by		
Owner's capital		10,000
Profit retained		8,700
Long-term loan		10,000
		28,700

4. From Parkwood & Company accounts:

Sources and applications of funds statement

		£
Cash and liquid funds at start of year		(660)
(cash + overdraft = £4,340 – £5,500)		
Sources of funds		
Trading, ie last year's profit before tax	15,530	
New long-term loan	8,000	23,530
		22,870

Application (uses of funds)
Purchase of fixed assets   11,500
Tax paid   2,960

Increases in working capital   £
  Stock (£14,650 – £9,920)   4,730
  Debtors (£38,800 – £24,730)   14,070
  Creditors* (£29,140 – £24,000)   (5,140)   13,660
                                                                 ————

                                                                  28,120
Cash and liquid funds at year end   (5,250)
  (cash + overdraft = £750 – £6,000)   ————

                                                                  22,870

*Don't forget creditors are people you have borrowed from, so we have to knock that extra source of money off new working capital to see how much more funds are tied up.

Chapter 4

1. To make a satisfactory return on capital employed and to maintain a sound financial position.

2. (a) Lower expenses; (b) Lower finance charge and tax; (c) Lower fixed assets; (d) Lower working capital.

3. (a) A personal goal – or budget; (b) This year against last; (c) Another business's performance – or an industry average.

4. (a) Unadjusted sales ratios.

Year	Sales £	Sales growth £	Sales growth ratio %
1	100,000	–	–
2	130,000	30,000	30
3	160,000	30,000	23

(b) Sales growth, adjusted for inflation
  (i) For year 1 sales now become 140/106 × £100,000 = £132,075
             2   140/124 × £130,000 = £146,774
             3   140/140 × £160,000 = £160,000

(ii) Year	Adjusted sales £	Adjusted sales growth £	Adjusted sales-growth ratio %
1	132,075	–	–
2	146,774	14,699	11.1
3	160,000	13,226	9.0

Chapter 5

		Year 1	Year 2
1. (a) Return on total capital employed	=	$\dfrac{13,222}{25,700}$	$\dfrac{17,960}{44,730}$
	=	51.4%	39.5%
Return on shareholders' capital	=	$\dfrac{7,213}{15,700}$	$\dfrac{11,030}{26,730}$
	=	46%	41%
Gearing	=	$\dfrac{10,000}{15,700}$	$\dfrac{18,000}{26,730}$
	=	0.64:1	0.67:1
Times interest earned	=	$\dfrac{13,222}{1,200}$	$\dfrac{17,690}{2,160}$
	=	11X	8X
Gross profit	=	$\dfrac{39,890}{249,340}$	$\dfrac{55,450}{336,030}$
	=	15.9%	16.5%
Operating profit	=	$\dfrac{13,222}{249,340}$	$\dfrac{17,690}{336,030}$
	=	5.3%	5.2%
Net profit after tax	=	$\dfrac{7,213}{249,340}$	$\dfrac{11,030}{336,030}$
	=	2.9%	3.3%

Chapter 6

1. Overtrading is the term used to describe a business which is expanding beyond its capacity to get additional working capital resources. As sales expand, the money tied up in stocks and customers' credit grows rapidly. Pressure also comes from suppliers who want payment for the ever-increasing supply of raw materials. The natural escape valve for pressures on working capital is an overdraft (or a substantial increase in the current one). Unfortunately, many small or expanding businesses do not have a financial planning or control system, so steps to secure additional working capital are often not taken until too late.

2. (a) The current ratio = $\dfrac{38,990}{31,960}$ = 1.22:1; $\dfrac{54,200}{39,640}$ = 1.37:1

 (b) The quick ratio = $\dfrac{29,070}{31,960}$ = 0.91:1; $\dfrac{39,550}{39,640}$ = 0.99:1

 (c) The average collection period =

 $\dfrac{24,730}{249,340}$ × 365 = 36 days; $\dfrac{38,800}{336,030}$ × 365 = 42 days

 (d) Average days' stock held =

 $\dfrac{9,920}{209,450}$ × 365 = 17 days; $\dfrac{14,650}{280,580}$ × 365 = 19 days

 (e) Circulation of working capital =

 $\dfrac{249,340}{7,030}$ = 35X $\dfrac{336,030}{14,560}$ = 23X

3. Without knowing the nature of the business any comment is conjectural. The facts, however, are that working capital has increased, largely as a result of having to finance higher stock levels and more debtors. The debtors are, on average, taking six days longer to pay. This represents an extra working capital requirement of £5,524 in the second year:

$$\frac{(336,030 \times 6)}{365}$$

As this sum is a fifth of the whole capital base of the business in the preceding year (£25,700), it seems too much to accept from 'careless' control of working capital. It has also contributed to the lower ROCE figures. (See Question 1 in Chapter 5.)

Chapter 7

1. Testing the internal rate of return (IRR) deduced by interpolation:

Year	Net cash flow £	Present-value factor at 23%	Net present value £
0	(7,646)	1.000	(7,646)
1	3,000	0.813	2,439
2	4,000	0.661	2,644
3	5,000	0.538	2,690
		Present value	7,773
		Net present value	127

	£	Present value factor at 24%	£
0	(7,646)	1.000	(7,646)
1	3,000	0.806	2,418
2	4,000	0.650	2,600
3	5,000	0.524	2,620
		Present value	7,638
		Net present value	(8)

This proves the IRR is between 23 and 24 per cent, which is quite accurate enough for capital appraisal purposes.

---

*The business depends on the success or failure of this key post, so over most of the first year this must be viewed as a fixed cost even if the salesperson is changed.

2. Using the 10 per cent trial rate would produce the following:

$$\text{IRR} \quad = 10 + \left[\frac{(2,140)}{2,140 + 126} \times (25 - 10) \right] \%$$

$$= 10 + 14.2 = 24.2$$

This is above the proven IRR rate of 23 per cent and so demonstrates that the wider the interest band used for interpolation, the less accurate the calculated IRR. The converse must also be true. Nevertheless, this degree of accuracy would be quite satisfactory for most capital appraisal work.

3. (a) **Machine A**

Year	Cash out £	Cash in £	Net £	10%	Net present value £	15%	Net present value £
0	12,500	–	(12,500)	1.000	(12,500)	1.000	(12,500)
1		2,000	2,000	0.909	1,818	0.870	1,740
2		4,000	4,000	0.826	3,304	0.756	3,024
3		5,000	5,000	0.751	3,755	0.658	3,290
4		2,500	2,500	0.683	1,708	0.572	1,430
5		3,500	3,500	0.621	2,173	0.497	1,739
					12,758		11,223
			Net present value		258		(1,277)

Machine B

Year	Cash out £	Cash in £	Net £	10%	Net present value £	15%	Net present value £
0	15,000	–	(15,000)	1.000	(15,000)	1.000	(15,000)
1		3,000	3,000	0.909	2,727	0.870	2,610
2		6,000	6,000	0.826	4,956	0.765	4,590
3		5,000	5,000	0.751	3,755	0.658	3,290
4		3,000	3,000	0.683	2,049	0.572	1,716
5		4,500	4,500	0.621	2,794	0.497	2,236
					16,281		14,442
			Net present value		1,281		(558)

(b) **Machine A**

Internal rate of return $= 10\% + \left[\dfrac{258}{258 + 1,277} \times (15 - 10) \right]$

$= 10\% + (0.168 \times 5) = 10\% + 0.84\%$
$= 10.84\%$

Machine B

Internal rate of return $= 10\% + \left[\dfrac{1,281}{1,281 + 558} \times (15 - 10) \right]$

$= 10\% + (0.697 \times 5) = 10\% + 3.5\%$
$= 13.5\%$

(c) Profitability index for Machine A $= \dfrac{12,750}{12,500} = 1.02$

Profitability index for Machine B $= \dfrac{16,281}{15,000} = 1.09$

(d) Machine B is the choice. It comes ahead in all financial considerations: higher positive net present value at the 10 per cent discount level, lower negative net present value at the 15 per cent discount level, higher internal rate of return. And finally, as the projects call for different sizes of initial investment, the profitability index must be taken into consideration. Once again Machine B comes out better.

Chapter 8

1. Margin of safety calculations:

	Company A £	Company B £
Total sales	100,000	100,000
− Break-even point	53,330	36,360
= Margin of safety	46,670	63,640
Margin of safety as a percentage of sales	46.7%	63.6%

2. (a) *Break-even point (BEP)*

Fixed costs	£	*Unit variable costs*	£
Car	1,500	Sales commission	5
Salary*	5,000	Unit buy-in price	30
Office	3,500	Unit installation costs	10
Other	4,500	Sundry variable costs	5
Advertising	2,000		
Total	16,500	Total	50

$$\text{BEP} = \frac{\text{Fixed costs}}{\text{Selling price} - \text{Unit variable costs}}$$

$$= \frac{16,500}{100 - 50} = \frac{16,500}{50} = 330 \text{ units.}$$

(b) *Break-even profit point (BEPP)*

$$\text{BEPP} = \frac{\text{Fixed cost} + \text{Profitability objective}}{\text{Selling price} - \text{Variable costs}}$$

$$\frac{16,500 + 10,000}{100 - 50} = \frac{26,500}{50}$$

$$= 530 \text{ units.}$$

(c) *Calculating new selling price*

$$400 = \frac{26,500}{\text{Selling price} - 50}$$

$$\text{Selling price} = 50 + \frac{26,500}{400} = £116.25$$

(d) *New cost structure*

Fixed	£	Variable	£
Car	2,500	Unit buy-in price	30
Sales salary	8,000	Sundry variable costs	5
Office	3,500		
Advertising	2,000		
Installation engineer	6,000		
Other	4,500		
Total	26,500		35

(i) *Break-even point*

$$\text{BEP} = \frac{26,500}{100 - 35} = 407 \text{ units}$$

(ii) *Break-even profit point*

$$\text{BEPP} = \frac{36,500}{65} \quad 561 \text{ units}$$

(iii) *Calculating new selling price*

$$400 = \frac{36,500}{\text{Selling price} - 35}$$

$$\text{Selling price} = 35 + \frac{36,500}{400} = £126.25$$

Useful organisations for help and advice

Business Link

Business Link is a nationwide network of around 220 advice centres. It provides affordable advice to small- and medium-sized firms. Each Business Link has two core services, the Information Service and the Advice Service.

The Information Service provides a single, local point of access to information on any business query. Whilst that information may come from a wide range of sources, such as Chambers of Commerce, local government or even banks, Business Link provides a single direct route to such information.

Business Link also provides tailored, on-the-spot advice from a range of specialist advisers covering such fields as; export, finance, innovation, technology, design, marketing and training.

Pricing structures vary between Business Links, but the fundamental premise is that services should be accessible and affordable. The Business Link Nationwide signpost number is 0345 567765.

Organisations

Accounting Web

Web site: www.accountingweb.co.uk

Accounting Web offers a range of accountancy resources, including an online weekly newsletter, a company-information search tool, access to *Key Note Executive Summaries*, and a directory of over 2,000 accountancy firms in the United Kingdom.

Association of British Credit Unions
Holyoak House
Hanover Street
Manchester M60 0AS

Tel: 0161 832 3694
Fax: 0161 832 3706
E-mail: info@abcul.org

Association of Chartered Certified Accountants
29 Lincoln's Inn Fields
London WC2A 3EE

Tel: 020 7242 6855
Fax: 020 7831 8054
Web site: www.acca.org.uk

Board of Inland Revenue
Press Office
Somerset House
Strand
London WC2R 1LB

Tel: 020 7438 6692
Fax: 020 7438 7541
Web site: www.inlandrevenue.gov.uk

British Chambers of Commerce
Manning House
22 Carlisle Place
London SW1P 1JA

Tel: 020 7565 2000
Web site: www.britishchambers.org.uk

The British Chambers of Commerce Web site provides information about their activities, as well as press releases and links to local Chambers of Commerce sites.

British Venture Capital Association (BVCA)
Essex House
12–13 Essex Street
London WC2R 3AA

Tel: 020 7240 3846
Fax: 020 7240 3849
Web site: www.bvca.co.uk

The BVCA Web site provides extensive information on venture capital in the UK and on the services of the BVCA, which represents every major source of venture capital in the United Kingdom.

Business Clubs UK

Web site: www.businessclub.co.uk

Business Clubs UK provides contact information for over 600 business clubs, groups and associations throughout the United Kingdom, as well as links to other business sites.

Business Credit Management UK
Mariners House
24 Nelsons Gardens
Hedge End
Southampton SO30 2NE

Tel: 01489 787541
Web site: www.creditman.co.uk

This commercial site provides a comprehensive resource for business credit, including news, information on company formations and insolvencies, and legal resources.

Business in the Community
44 Baker Street
London W1M 1DH

Tel: 020 7224 1600
Fax: 020 7486 1700
Web site: www.bitc.org.uk

Business Link London
6 New Bridge Street
London EC4V 6AB

Tel: 020 7557 7300
Fax: 020 7557 7301
Web site: www.bll.org.uk
E-mail: info@london.businesslink.co.uk

The Business Link Web site offers an overview of the Business Link
network of advice centres, including location details for local offices,
details of available services and advice, and a search engine that is
based on an index of accredited UK business sites.

Business Money Ltd
Strode House
10 Leigh Road
Street
Somerset BA16 OHA

Tel: 01458 841112
Fax: 01458 841286
Web site: www.business-money.com

The online version of *Business Money* provides an independent review
of finance and banking for business, and offers articles from the
current edition plus links to pages supplying current financial news.

Business Names Registration plc
Somerset House
Temple St
Birmingham B2 5DN

Tel: 0121 643 0227
Fax: 0121 678 9001
Web site: www.bnr.plc.uk

For a small fee, the Business Names Register will search more than 3 million business names and 600,000 registered trademarks to ensure that your name does not conflict with any other. It will also help you to ensure your own business name is legal and protected. It publishes a newsletter to communicate any changes in UK/EU legislation that may affect names and ownership, will obtain permission if your name contains a restricted word or phrase, and will pay litigation costs in order to protect your name if required.

CCTA Government Information Service

Web site: www.open.gov.uk

Maintained by the Central Computer and Telecommunications Agency, this Web site provides access to over 400 UK public-sector Web sites, including the G7 Information Network for Small and Medium-Sized Enterprises.

Chartered Institute of Management Accountants
63 Portland Place
London W1N 6AB

Tel: 020 7637 2311
Fax: 020 7631 5309
Web site: www.cimaglobal.com

Companies House
PO Box 29019
21 Bloomsbury Street
London WC1B 3XD

Tel: 0292 038 0801
Fax: 0292 038 0517
Web site: www.companies-house.gov.uk/

The register of companies in the United Kingdom provides details about itself and its services on its Web site, together with extensive information and guidance for anyone setting up and running a limited company. Companies House is responsible for company registration in the United Kingdom. It also has a key role in providing information about British companies. The Web site contains a free information section of company names and addresses and disqualified directors. There are numerous guidance notes covering a wide range of topics, and many of the administrative forms are available online.

Confederation of British Industry
Centre Point
103 New Oxford Street
London WC1A 1DU

Tel: 020 7379 7400
Fax: 020 7240 1578
Web site: www.cbi.org.uk

The official Web site of the Confederation of British Industry (CBI) provides information on business in the UK and the organisation itself, including press releases, trend surveys, and a searchable database of articles from *CBI News.*

Cranfield School of Management
Cranfield
Bedford MK43 0AL

Tel: 01234 751122
Fax: 01234 751806
Web site: www.cranfield.ac.uk

Cranfield provides basic financial-management training programmes for owner-managers in small- and medium-sized firms in their Lifetime Learning for Growing Businesses programmes.

Department of Trade and Industry
1 Victoria Street
London SW1 0ET

Tel: 020 7215 5000
Fax: 020 7215 6446
Web site: www.dti.gov.uk

The Department of Trade and Industry provides information about its activities and resources for UK business and industry, including news, advice and regulatory guidance.

Dosh Software Ltd
PO Box 118
Horsham
West Sussex RH13 6FN

Tel: 01403 273590
Fax: 01403 210792
Freephone: 0800 0264666
Web site: www.dosh.co.uk
E-mail: sales@dosh.co.uk

This small business specialises in accounting software for the self-employed and businesses with less than 10 employees. DOSH Cashbook assumes no bookkeeping knowledge, but provides help through onscreen steps and a comprehensive manual. The software allows users to produce a complete record of all receipts and payments, a cash-flow summary, a VAT account and bank reconciliation statements for any period, printing reports on A4 paper. Trial versions of the software can be downloaded from the Web site.

Durham University Business School
Mill Hill Lane
Durham DH1 3LB

Tel: 0191 374 2211
Fax: 0191 374 3748
Web site: www.dur.ac.uk/udbs

Enterprise Advisory Service

Web site: www.govgrants.com

This commercial site provides information on business grants for UK companies, including news, eligibility criteria and details of grant sources.

Exports Credits Guarantee Department (ECGD)
PO Box 2200
2 Exchange Tower
Harbour Exchange Square
London E14 9GS

Tel: 020 7512 7000
Fax: 020 7215 7649
Web site: www.ecgd.gov.uk

Factors and Discounters Association
Administration Office
2nd Floor
Boston House
The Little Green
Richmond
Surrey TW9 1QE

Tel: 020 8332 9955
Fax: 020 8332 2585
Web site: www.factors.org.uk

Federation of Small Businesses
Whittle Way
Blackpool Business Park
Blackpool
Lancs FY4 2FE

Tel: 01253 336000
Fax: 01253 348046
Web site: www.fsb.org.uk

Finance and Leasing Association
Imperial House
15–19 Kingsway
London WC2B 6UN

Tel: 020 7836 6511
Fax: 020 7420 9600
Web site: www.fla.org.uk
E-mail: info@fla.org.uk

Greater London Enterprise Ltd
28 Park Street
London SE1 9EQ
Tel: 020 7403 0300
Fax: 020 7403 1742
Web site: www.gle.co.uk
E-mail: enterprise@gle.co.uk
E-mail: contact@gle.co.uk

Inland Revenue

Web site: www.inlandrevenue.gov.uk/home

The Inland Revenue provides information on UK taxation, including online versions of advice leaflets and tax forms, details on self-assessment and answers to frequently asked questions The Inland Revenue Web site features news and information on tax and National Insurance matters in the UK. It is easy to use and has a whole section devoted to 'Tax for Business', which contains information on self-assessment and corporation-tax self-assessment, the construction-industry scheme, rates, allowances, press releases, tax offices, helplines and orderlines. You can also access the New Business Starter Pack, forms, help sheets, leaflet and booklets.

Institute of Chartered Accountants in England and Wales
PO Box 433
Chartered Accountants Hall
Moorgate Place
London EC2P 2BJ

Tel: 020 7920 8100
Fax: 020 7920 8699
Web site: www.icaew.co.uk

The Institute of Chartered Accountants in England and Wales (ICAEW) Web site provides accountancy news and information, together with the full text of ICAEW reports on accounting in business, self-assessment taxation, and other subjects.

Institute of Chartered Accountants of Scotland
27 Queen Street
Edinburgh EH2 2LA

Tel: 0131 225 5673
Fax: 0131 225 3813
Web site: www.icas.org.uk

Institute of Company Accountants
40 Tyndalls Park Road
Bristol BS8 1PL

Tel: 01179 738261
Fax: 01179 238292

Institute of Directors
116 Pall Mall
London SW1Y 5ED
Tel: 020 7839 1233
Fax: 020 7930 9060
Web site: www.iod.co.uk

Intuit Service Centre
Freepost
SCE 127
Swindon
Wilts SN5 8ZZ

Tel: 0800 585058
Fax: 0845 6011571
Web site: www.intuit.co.uk

Intuit provides a full range of accounting software for small firms.

Kelly's

Web site: www.kellys.co.uk/

The official Web site of the business directory *Kelly's* offers a searchable database of over 12,000 UK companies, together with useful contacts and links to other business information; registration is required.

London Society of Chartered Accountants
15 Basinghall Street
London EC2A

Tel: 020 7726 2722
Fax: 020 7776 6930
Web site: www.lsca.co.uk

London Stock Exchange
Old Broad Street
London EC2N 1HP

Tel: 020 7797 4404
Fax: 020 7797 2001
Web site: www.londonstockexchange.com

National Business Angels Network
40–42 Cannon Street
London EC14N 6JJ

Tel: 020 7329 2929
Fax: 020 7329 2626
Web site: www.nban.com

The National Business Angels Network commercial Web site provides information on LINC (an organisation sponsored by several UK banks, which aims to introduce investors to businesses seeking growth and start-up capital) and includes details on its services and regional offices.

NatWest Bank

Web site: www.natwest.com

This commercial site from NatWest Bank provides a section containing news and information for small businesses, together with a business start-up planner and a business angels service linking businesses with potential investors.

Princes Trust
18 Park Square East
London NW1 4LH

Tel: 020 7543 1234
Fax: 020 7543 1200
Web site: www.princes-trust.org.uk

The business start-up arm of the Prince's Trust helps young people aged between 18 and 30 who are unemployed, under-employed or of limited means to start their own business. A last-resort funder, it offers low-interest business loans, test marketing grants, advice and other assistance such as discounted exhibition space.

Sage Group Plc
Sage House
Benton Park Road
Newcastle upon Tyne NE7 7LZ

Tel: 0191 255 3000
Fax: 0191 255 0308
Web site: www.sage.com

Sage offers a comprehensive range of accounting software for small firms.

Scottish Enterprise

Tel: 0845 6078787
Web site: www.scottish-enterprise.com

The economic development agency for Scotland provides a wealth of information for businesses in Scotland, including information on business-improvement schemes, trade and export, and local advice centres.

Small Firms Loan Guarantee Section
SME Policy Directorate
Department of Trade and Industry
Level 2
St Mary's House
c/o Moorfoot
Sheffield S1 4PQ

Tel: 0114 259 7308/9
Fax: 0114 259 7316
Web site: www.businessadviceonline.org

The Stationery Office

Web site: www.hmso.gov.uk/

The Stationery Office provides details of all Acts and Statutory Instruments that relate to business, including the all-important Companies Act.

Companies Act 1989 (c. 40)

Web site: http://194.128.65.3/acts/summary/01989040.htm

A summarised version of the Companies Act 1989, together with an order form for the full printed version.

Ulster Factors Ltd
7 North Street
Belfast BT1 1NH

Tel: 01232 324522
Fax: 01232 230336

Venture Capital Report
Magdalen Centre
Oxford Science Park
Oxford OX4 4GA

Tel: 01865 784411
Fax: 01865 784412

E-mail: vcr@vcrnet.unet.com

This commercial site aims to link investors with entrepreneurial businesses seeking capital and includes a list of current investment opportunities, as well as details of how to have your project featured in the report.

Venture Site

Web site: www.venturesite.co.uk

This commercial site provides an online marketplace for small companies needing investors. Registration and a small fee are required to place an advertisement for investors, but it is free to browse the lists of ventures and 'business angels'.

Further reading

Chapters 1 to 3

Bertram, D and Taylor, D (1997) *The Allied Dunbar Business Tax and Law Handbook*, Prentice-Hall, London

Foreman, A (2000) *The Allied Dunbar Business Tax Handbook*, Prentice-Hall, London

Myddleton, D (1995) *Essence of Financial Management*, Prentice-Hall, Herts

Myddleton, D, and Reid, W (2000) *The Meaning of Company Accounts*, Gower Press, Cardiff

Parker, R H (1999) *An Insight Into Management Accounting*, Penguin, London

Chapter 8

Czarnecki, M (1999) *Managing by Measuring*, Amacom, New York

Sizer, J (1989) *An Insight into Management Accounting*, revised 2nd edn, Penguin, London

Chapters 9 and 10

Barrow, C (2001) *The Business Plan Workbook*, 4th edn, Kogan Page, London

Finch, B (1998) *Business Plans*, Kogan Page, London

Kotler, P (1999) *Marketing Management*, millennium edition, Prentice-Hall, Herts (one of the most lucid and comprehensive books on the subject)

Chapters 11 and 12

Barrow, C (2000), *How to Survive the E-Downturn*, John Wiley, London

Drucker, P F (1999) *Managing for Results*, Butterworth-Heinemann, London

Kirkland, K and Howard, S (1998) *Simple and Practical Bookkeeping*, Kogan Page, London

Index

References in italic indicate figures or tables

Index of advertisers

Business Enterprise Guides

Published in association with *The Sunday Times*
and the Institute of Directors

The Business Plan Workbook, Fourth Edition
Colin Barrow, Paul Barrow and Robert Brown

*The Business Enterprise Handbook: A complete guide to achieving
profitable growth for all entrepreneurs and SMEs* (forthcoming)
Colin Barrow, Robert Brown and Liz Clarke

E-Business for the Small Business: Making a profit from the Internet
(forthcoming)
John G Fisher

Starting a Successful Business, Fourth Edition (forthcoming)
Michael J Morris

Successful Marketing for the Small Business: A practical guide, Fifth
Edition (forthcoming)
Dave Patten

All titles are available from good bookshops. To obtain further information, please contact the publisher at the following address:

Kogan Page Ltd
120 Pentonville Road
London N1 9JN
Tel: 020 7278 0433
Fax: 020 7837 6348
www.kogan-page.co.uk

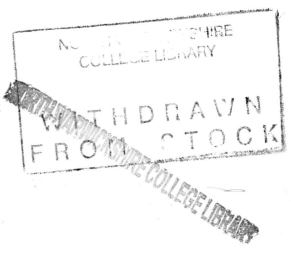